THE
Night Sky

AN OBSERVERS GUIDE

Dennis L. Mammana

MALLARD
PRESS

A FRIEDMAN GROUP BOOK
Published by MALLARD PRESS
An Imprint of BDD Promotional Book Company, Inc.
666 Fifth Avenue
New York, N.Y. 10103

ISBN 0-7924-5689-0

THE NIGHT SKY
An Observer's Guide
was prepared and produced by
Michael Friedman Publishing Group, Inc.
15 West 26th Street
New York, New York 10010

Editor: Nathaniel Marunas
Art Director: Jeff Batzli
Designer: Jill Ruscoll
Photography Editor: Anne Price

Color separations by United South Sea Graphic Art Co., Ltd.
Printed and bound in Hong Kong by Leefung-Asco Printers Ltd.

Dedication

To Mrs. Uhler and Mr. Wagner.
Thank you for helping to turn my eyes skyward.

Contents

Part I:

A Naked Eye Universe

Part II:

A Close-up Look

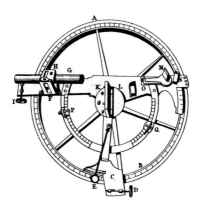

Part One

A Naked Eye Universe

Introduction

© FPG International

    What do you see when you look into the night sky? Stars—thousands of them—scattered across the darkened heavens. Some stars are bright, and others are dim. Some twinkle, while others shine steadily. Some stars even appear to be different colors, such as orange, white, or blue.

    Clearly, the sky doesn't always appear to be the same; in fact, it seems different from night to night—even from hour to hour. Sometimes the Big Dipper is visible, and other times it is not. Sometimes the "evening star" shines brightly in the western sky at sunset, and other times it appears in the east.

Occasionally we see a faint, hazy band of light—the Milky Way—stretching from horizon to horizon. Now and then, a star appears to drift by slowly through the others, perhaps brightening and dimming, before gradually fading from view on the opposite side of the sky. Sometimes we'll see a falling star, one that drops suddenly out of the sky in a fiery burst of light.

With so many variables, it's no wonder that the average person is confused when gazing upward toward the night sky for the first time. This book will help you understand the stars and planets and, more importantly, show you how to enjoy the wonders of the universe from your own backyard.

Viewing an Ancient Sky

The sky we see today is essentially the same that our ancestors saw centuries—even millennia—ago. With little or no equipment, these people watched the sky night after night, and discovered "patterns" that were repeated again and again. But understanding these patterns did not come quickly.

Many of these early observers watched the skies to understand the will of the gods, whom they believed controlled the universe. Some searched for connections between Earth and heaven, thinking that specific celestial occurrences might point to specific events to follow on Earth. Still others tried to understand the physical reality of the universe through measurement and mathematics.

From their observations, the ancients believed that the sun, stars, moon, and planets all wheeled around the Earth in an endless cycle. They believed that the Earth occupied the center of the universe.

It was not until the sixteenth century that Polish astronomer Copernicus dared to challenge the wisdom of the ages with the notion that the sun, not the Earth, occupied the center of the universe. Copernicus showed mathematically that the Earth was merely one of the five planets known at the time that orbited the sun, and that the sky wheeling about us was merely an illusion caused by the Earth's position and motion. Unfortunately, since Copernicus had no observational proof to support his theories, few regarded his ideas as little more than a curious mathematical trick.

It was not long, however, before observational proof came into being, thanks to the invention of the telescope. While it is believed that the first telescope came from Holland, it was Italian scientist Galileo Galilei who

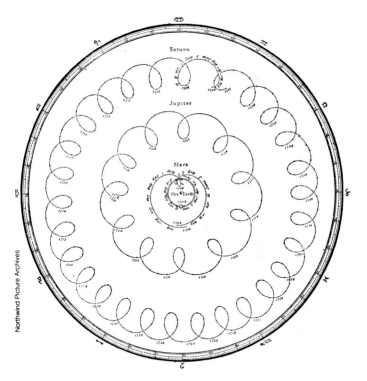

Northwind Picture Archives

Because they envisioned the Earth at the center of the solar system, the ancients required a complex pattern of orbits to explain planetary motion in the sky. Copernicus simplified matters by placing the sun at the center.

From left to right: Copernicus, Galileo, and Newton overturned commonly held concepts of the universe.

built and aimed his own telescope toward the heavens, and began the first comprehensive and systematic study of the universe.

Galileo soon discovered that the Milky Way was composed of millions and billions of individual stars, and that their blended light produced its amorphous appearance. He found that the moon was pocked with craters and rilles, cracks and mountains. He also used mathematics to show that some of those mountains were more than 4 miles (6.4km) high. He found that Jupiter had four moons orbiting it, and he mapped their positions from night to night. He also learned that the brilliant planet Venus actually mimicked the moon, showing itself in phases that ranged from thin crescent to quarter to full, depending on its position relative to the sun and Earth. Through these concerted observations, Galileo effectively proved that the Earth was not the center of the universe but was instead one of many worlds scattered through space.

Over the years, telescopes were made bigger and more powerful. Astronomers soon found that the sun was not at the universe's center either, but was, in fact, only one star of hundreds of billions of similar stars making up the spiral galaxy we call the Milky Way. In addition, the Milky Way was soon recognized as a small to average-sized galaxy that resides in a cluster of galaxies somewhere in a universe extending 100,000 billion billion miles (160,000 billion billion km).

Viewing an Ancient Sky Through Modern Eyes

Isaac Newton once said: "If I have seen farther it is because I've stood on the shoulders of giants." We, too, stand on the shoulders of giants, for we gaze into the night sky with a far better perspective than those of ages past. We no longer view the moon as a perfect white sphere since we watched humans walk its dusty and cratered surface. We have seen the rings of Saturn, the immense cloud systems of Jupiter, the bizarre moons of Uranus and Neptune—courtesy of a robot spacecraft named *Voyager*. We don't shy away from lively party discussions of such things as extraterrestrial life, black holes, and the Big Bang.

Today, we recognize that the Earth is a tiny part of a vast cosmos. Our nearest neighbor in space, the moon, lies at an incredible 240,000 miles (384,500km) from us. Our sun is 93 million miles (148,800,000km) away. The planets lie hundreds of millions of miles beyond us; Neptune, for example, lies some 3 billion miles (4.8 billion km) away.

Yet these planets are our neighbors, for the stars are even farther away from us. Proxima Centauri, the nearest star visible to those in Earth's Southern Hemisphere, lies some 26 trillion miles (41.5 trillion km) away. Beyond Proxima Centauri, some 200 billion stars make up the swirling galaxy we know as the Milky Way galaxy, which stretches some 600,000 trillion miles (960,000 trillion km) from end to end. Beyond the Milky Way are scattered even more galaxies—as far as the largest telescopes can see—some as distant as 100 billion trillion miles (160 billion trillion km).

No human can ever hope to comprehend such huge

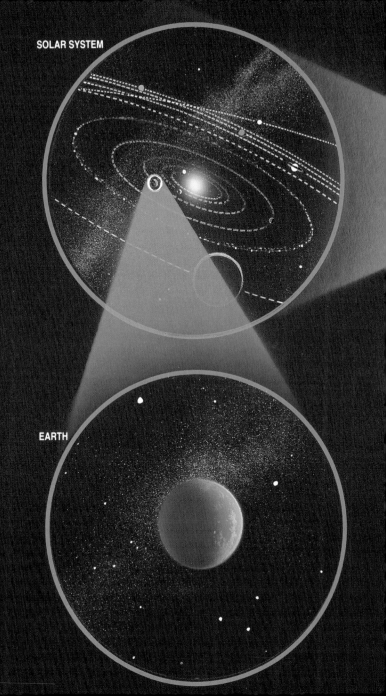

SOLAR SYSTEM

EARTH

MILKY WAY
GALAXY

UNIVERSE

Our tiny planet Earth orbits the sun, one
of two hundred billion stars in the Milky
Way galaxy. The Milky Way, in turn, is
but one of hundreds of billions of galaxies that make up the universe.

numbers, so astronomers use the speed of light to help gauge cosmic distances. Light is the fastest-travelling substance known: it travels at a speed of 186,000 miles (297,600km) per second through the vacuum of space. Yet, even at that speed, light takes a significant amount of time to travel from space to the point where we on Earth can observe it.

For example, moonlight takes about 1.3 seconds to travel the 240,000 miles (384,500km) to the Earth. From the sun, light takes some 8.3 minutes to get here; that is, sunlight is already 8 minutes and 19 seconds old when it lights our world. From Proxima Centauri, light takes 4.3 years to get here, so we are actually seeing the star as it was 4.3 years ago. In effect, it lies 4.3 "light-years" away. In other words, the farther we peer into space, the farther back into time we look. The Milky Way galaxy stretches some 100,000 light-years from end to end, and the farthest known objects may lie some 15 or 18 billion light-years away. Again, the numbers become incomprehensible.

Perhaps the best way to grasp these distances is with a scale model of the universe. If the sun were the size of a basketball, the Earth, by comparison, would be the size of a pinhead nearly 100 feet (30m) away. The moon would be a smaller pinhead located about an inch (2.5cm) from the Earth. Pluto would be an invisible speck nearly a mile (1.6km) away from the sun, and Proxima Centauri would be represented by a softball 4,000 miles (6,400km) away. Also on this greatly reduced scale, the Milky Way would stretch for 100 million miles (160 million km)—the universe far beyond that!

♦

This is indeed a marvelous universe. Perhaps even more amazing is that the entire universe is right outside your door. To experience it costs nothing; no equipment is needed to enjoy and understand the cosmos. In fact, examples of virtually every type of object and phenomenon in the universe are available from your backyard—if you know when, where, and how to look.

Chapter 1

Before It Gets Dark

© Richard E. Hill

To get a good view of the heavens, all you really need are your eyes. But if you wish to be comfortable, or if you really want to learn something from your observations, you will need to consider several important points.

The first thing to think about is your observing site. Does it have a good, dark, and clear view of the sky? City lights tend to scatter upward and wash out the fainter stars. This might be desirable as you begin to learn your way around the sky, but it won't be long before you will want an observation site in the country or mountains, far from the devastation of light pollution.

Above: The sunset is a spectacular celestial event that you can see on most days.

Another point to consider is the position of the moon. If the moon is up, you may not wish to search for faint stars and constellations, since its light will also wash them from view. With a bright moon in the sky, it would not be worth the long drive to a dark-sky site. You may wish instead to concentrate on the brighter stars, planets, and constellations. Plan your observing session accordingly.

At Sunset

Astronomers generally set up their evening's session before it gets dark, especially if the site is new. They often use this time to become accustomed to the land and to watch the sunset. During this time of day, brightnesses and colors can change within minutes: if you take your eyes off the sky for any length of time, you will surely miss something fascinating. To understand why sky colors change at sunset, you need to ask why the sky is blue in the first place.

Although we perceive the sun to shine with white light, it is actually composed of a spectrum of colors: red, orange, yellow, green, blue, and violet. The sky contains extremely small particles of gas that have an effect on these wavelengths of light; these gases "scatter" light, which means that they reflect light randomly around the sky. Not all colors interact in the same way with these gaseous molecules, however. The shortest wavelengths of sunlight are most susceptible to scattering, and since the blue wavelengths are the shortest in the spectrum, they interact most readily with the gaseous molecules, producing the sky's blue color.

Sunsets work in a similar fashion. Later in the afternoon, the Earth turns away from the sun, so the sunlight must pass through more atmosphere than it did at noon. Now the sunlight encounters more particles than it did before, and eventually only the longer wavelengths of light are able to reach us. This is why the sky changes from blue to yellow, then to orange, and finally to red. Furthermore, large amounts of particles in the

Stars begin to appear in the sky during twilight. They have been there all day, but the improved contrast at night makes them visible.

© John Sanford/Photo Network

atmosphere, such as dust, pollution, and volcanic ash, enhance sunsets because of the increased amount of interference.

As spectacular as sunsets can be, not all the action occurs in the western part of the sky. Just after sunset, cast your gaze toward the east and another celestial wonder will come into view. If the sky is clear, a large, dark purplish haze will appear low in the east just at dusk. This "haze" is the shadow of the Earth.

As the sun sets below the western horizon, part of its light is blocked by our planet and cannot reach the eastern sky. This part of the sky naturally appears darker than the rest; if you look carefully, you will notice that its top portion is reddish in color. The reason for this is that some of the reddened sunlight is penetrating the atmosphere and lighting up the boundary between shadow and light. Watch the shadow carefully and you will see it rise higher in the east as darkness falls. Eventually, it blends more and more into the general sky darkness, and becomes increasingly difficult to see.

The First Stars

Now is the time that the first stars begin to shine in the sky. They have been there all day, of course, but now the sky is dark enough for us to see them clearly. This is a good time to check out the sky for the evening's observing session.

One of the first things to notice is if there are clouds or any haze. Clouds and haze will tend to disappear from view after darkness has fallen, yet may critically affect your ability to see certain phenomena. This condition is known as the "transparency" of the sky.

Another factor to consider is how much the stars twinkle. This effect is known to astronomers as "scintillation," and has absolutely nothing to do with the stars themselves. This phenomenon occurs entirely within the Earth's atmosphere.

As a star's tiny beam of light enters the atmosphere, the wavering and moving currents of air bounce the beam around and make it appear to waver or twinkle. Stars also often may appear to sparkle in different colors as they twinkle. A star overhead, because its light passes

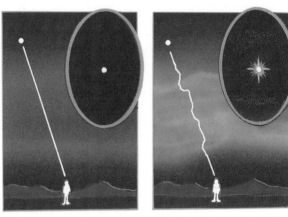

© Brian Sullivan

A star's twinkling is caused by atmospheric turbulence. On a bad night, stars sparkle wildly, sometimes even changing colors.

through much less atmosphere, tends to twinkle less than one near the horizon.

While scintillation is quite pretty to watch, it is devastating to stargazers, who must measure how severely stars are twinkling to learn how productive their night will be. Obviously, the steadier the atmosphere the better. The measure of the atmosphere's steadiness is called "seeing." To measure seeing, find a bright star high overhead. If it twinkles noticeably, the seeing is bad. If it shines with a steady light, the seeing is good.

A measure of the seeing determines, in part, how faint an object you will be able to see, and how much fine detail in the sky will be visible. If on a dark, moonless night, the seeing is excellent or good, you should explore some of the fainter and harder-to-see parts of the sky. If the seeing is fair or poor, you might wish to concentrate on brighter features of the sky.

Preserving Your Night Vision

As the night darkens, your eyes will slowly adjust to the changing light conditions. This is called "dark adaptation." As your pupils open wider to let in more light, you will find that you can see better in the darkness. You will need to remain dark adapted if you are going to see the sky well.

A simple experiment shows how dark adaptation works. Close your eyes for 20 to 30 minutes. Now, while standing in front of a bathroom mirror, open your eyes and watch what happens to your pupils. Having been in darkness for so long, they were opened wide to be able to gather more light. As light pours onto them, the pupils automatically and quickly close down to compensate. It may take another half hour for them to become dark adapted once again.

Dark adaptation is extremely easy to lose. Glancing toward a white flashlight shining on a piece of paper, the headlights of an oncoming car, or even a campfire can destroy your dark adaptation in only seconds, so avoid bright lights when stargazing. If you need to read

On a clear dark night, far from city lights, some two thousand stars can be seen with the unaided eye.

© Geoff Chester

or write notes, or find your way around, use only red light. You can make a red flashlight by covering a white one with red cellophane, or painting its bulb with red nail polish. This way you will be able to see everything around you and retain complete night vision.

Seeing the Unseeable

As darkness falls, fainter and fainter objects come into view. One trick astronomers use to see extremely faint detail is called "averted vision."

Averted vision uses the edges of the eye's retina rather than its center to see things that might otherwise be invisible. The central part of the retina contains color receptors, known as cones. Cones provide color to us, but need a lot of light to function. The outer part of the retina contains the black-and-white sensors, known as rods. These help us see when light is scarce, but provide us no color at all.

To see faint detail in the sky (or here on Earth, for that matter), use your rods instead of your cones. Don't look directly at a faint object; instead look slightly off to its side. This way, you'll put your rods to work and will see the object out of the corner of your eye. This is particularly useful in seeing and studying very faint celestial bodies.

Measuring the Sky

Measuring phenomena in the sky is impossible if we try to compare them to Earth-bound objects. For example, to say that something is the size of a baseball depends entirely on the baseball's distance from us. Likewise, to describe an object's speed as being comparable to that of an airplane depends on the airplane's distance from us. The best way to measure the sky is to use a unit of measurement that is totally independent of distance: the degree.

A degree is simply 1/360 of a circle. The horizon around you—the imaginary line between the sky and the ground—defines a circle and it, too, can be divided into 360 equal pieces, each 1 degree wide. The same is true with the sky.

Begin by holding your little finger up at arm's length; its width is approximately 1 degree. That means if you

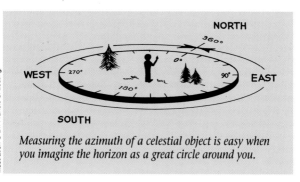

Measuring the azimuth of a celestial object is easy when you imagine the horizon as a great circle around you.

Illustration © Dr. Francis S. Lestingi

count how many little fingers it would take to make up the horizon, it should come out to about 360. A thumb held at arm's length is approximately 2 degrees across; a fist, about 10 degrees from thumb to little finger.

These, of course, are rough measures, depending on the size of your hand and the length of your arm, but you can determine them more exactly. First, measure the width of your measuring tool (perhaps a thumb). Then, measure its distance from your eye, making sure to keep the units the same. Divide its width by its distance, and multiply the total by 55. This will give you the approximate number of degrees it subtends.

With this angular measure, you can now describe more precisely how large something appears in the sky, how high it is above the horizon, and even how fast it appears to be moving—all without knowing its distance. Since a degree is a degree no matter how it is measured, it makes an excellent unit for communicating your observations with others.

Keeping Records

As you watch the skies and learn your way around, you will want to keep a record of your observations. This logbook doesn't have to be fancy—a simple tablet or notebook will do. The book will help you remember important details that you might otherwise forget.

When creating your logbook, be sure to include as much information as you can. Data might include the date, time, and number of the observing session; the sky conditions, including the seeing and transparency; any instruments you used to view the sky; who observed with you; what objects you observed; any unusual sights, including a complete description; drawings or photographs; the position and phase of the moon—in short, anything that might affect your observations and help answer future questions.

Using Star Maps

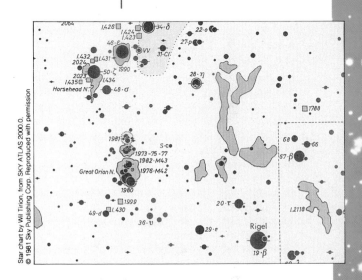

Making sense of the stars comes from recognizing their patterns. But finding those patterns is not always easy and can be terribly frustrating to the beginning stargazer. This is why a star map can be helpful. A star map is a re-creation of the night sky printed on paper. Some star maps are quite simple, while others are rather advanced; those on pages 28 to 31 are good choices for begin-

Above: Stars can be found and identified on maps of the sky. These maps can be as simple or as complex as necessary.

ning stargazers in the Northern Hemisphere. The maps on pages 32 to 35 are for Southern Hemisphere observers.

Since the sky changes constantly, each star map is printed to show the early evening sky for a certain season of the year. Each map is outlined by a circle that represents the horizon. At the map's center is a + mark that represents the overhead point in the sky, also known as the zenith. Along the circle are marked the cardinal directions: north, south, east, and west.

Reading a Star Map

To read a star map properly, hold it over your head and align its cardinal directions with those on the real horizon. If you have selected the proper map, it should correspond closely with the real sky of early evening.

The black dots on the map represent the stars—the bigger the dot the brighter the star. The words printed in lowercase letters (e.g., Polaris in the Northern Hemisphere; Antares in the Southern Hemisphere) are the names of brighter stars. Some of the dots are connected with dotted lines that represent easily recognizable groupings. Their names are printed in capital letters (e.g., LITTLE DIPPER in the Northern Hemisphere, SCORPIUS in the Southern Hemisphere). Don't be confused if you see bright objects that do not appear on your star map; they are probably planets.

There are two ways to use a star map. The first is to go from the sky to the map. Suppose a Northern Hemisphere observer is outdoors just after dark in summer and sees a bright star a third of the way between the southwestern horizon and the zenith. A quick glance at the correct star map shows that this star is named Arcturus, and lies within the grouping named Boötes. The same technique works for the Southern Hemisphere, but the stars seen are different (notable constellations for Southern Hemisphere observers include Crux and Centaurus).

The other way to use the map is to go from map to sky. Suppose, for example, you want to find the star named Altair. The same summer map shows it to lie about two thirds of the way from the zenith to the southeastern horizon. You can see it lying within the grouping known as Aquila.

Star Hopping

Another technique for finding find your way around the sky is called "star hopping." With this method, you can use stars and star groupings that you already know to find those you don't. Solid lines and arrowheads on the star map will help you along.

Suppose a Northern Hemisphere observer has already found the Big Dipper on a clear spring evening, high in the northern sky. Simply follow the two stars at the end of the Big Dipper's "bowl"—from its bottom to its top—and extend that line about five times the distance between them. You will soon encounter a bright star named Polaris. Polaris is also known as the North Star, and it is the point in the sky corresponding to the North Celestial Pole, the point directly above the Earth's north pole. A Southern Hemisphere observer has no similar star at the South Celestial Pole, although the Southern Cross is always visible.

You can even use the curve of the Big Dipper's handle to find two other stars. By following its curve, or "arc," you soon come to Arcturus, the brightest star in Boötes, the Herdsman. Continuing the curve onward past Arcturus takes you down toward Spica, the brightest star in Virgo, the Virgin.

The Big Dipper is a great star-hopping tool in the spring and summer months for Northern Hemisphere observers. Orion, the Hunter, can be used during winter and spring months in the Northern Hemisphere, and during summer and autumn months below the equator. Orion is most easily recognized by its four stars, which form a vertical rectangle, with three bright stars in a straight line across its middle. Follow these three stars to the east and you will come to Sirius, the brightest star in the nighttime sky. Follow them

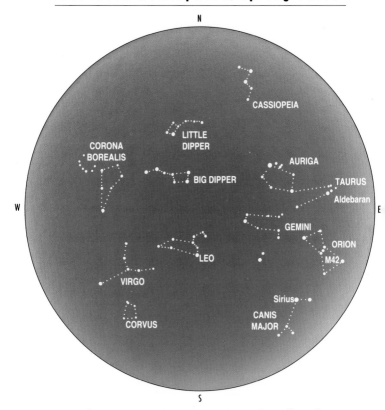

N

CASSIOPEIA

LITTLE
DIPPER

CORONA
BOREALIS

AURIGA

BIG DIPPER

TAURUS

Aldebaran

W   E

GEMINI

ORION

LEO   M42

VIRGO

Sirius

CORVUS

CANIS
MAJOR

S

Corvus

Cassiopeia

Northern Hemisphere/Summer Skies

CASSIOPEIA

Polaris

LITTLE DIPPER

CYGNUS

BIG DIPPER

LEO

CORONA BOREALIS

BOOTES

Arcturus

AQUILA

VIRGO

LIBRA

Spica

SAGITTARIUS

SCORPIUS

N

S

W

E

All starmaps © Brian Sullivan

Aquila

Scorpius

Northern Hemisphere/Autumn Skies

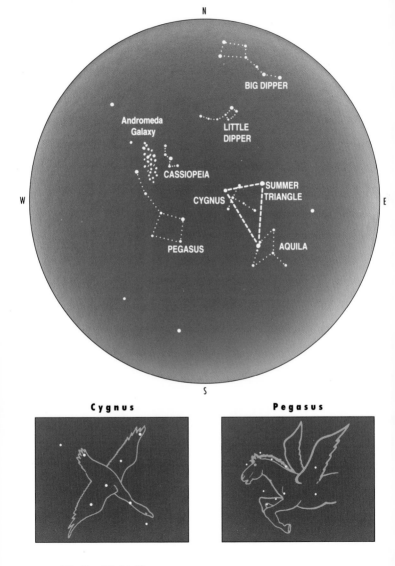

N

BIG DIPPER

LITTLE DIPPER

Andromeda Galaxy

CASSIOPEIA

W

CYGNUS

SUMMER TRIANGLE

E

PEGASUS

AQUILA

S

Cygnus

Pegasus

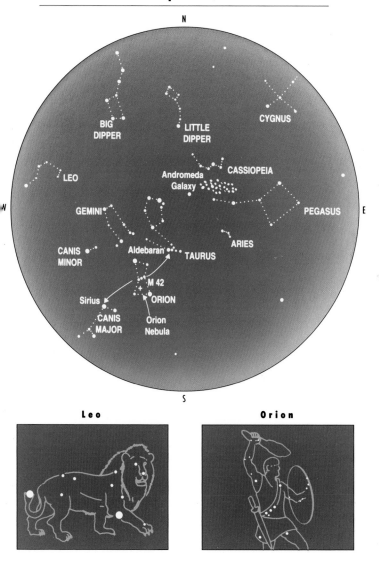

N

W

E

S

BIG DIPPER

LITTLE DIPPER

CYGNUS

LEO

Andromeda Galaxy

CASSIOPEIA

GEMINI

PEGASUS

CANIS MINOR

Aldebaran

TAURUS

ARIES

M 42

Sirius

ORION

CANIS MAJOR

Orion Nebula

Leo

Orion

Southern Hemisphere/Spring Skies

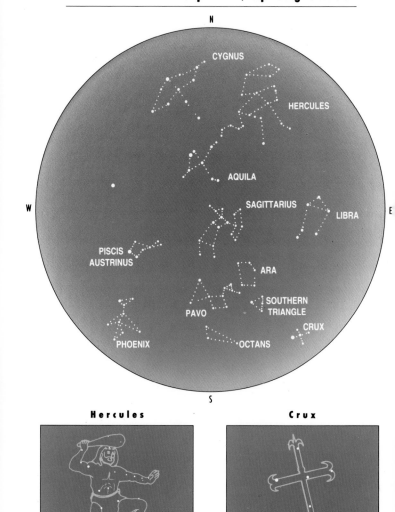

N

CYGNUS

HERCULES

AQUILA

SAGITTARIUS

LIBRA

W

E

PISCIS
AUSTRINUS

ARA

SOUTHERN
TRIANGLE

CRUX

PAVO

PHOENIX

OCTANS

S

Hercules

Crux

Southern Hemisphere/Summer Skies

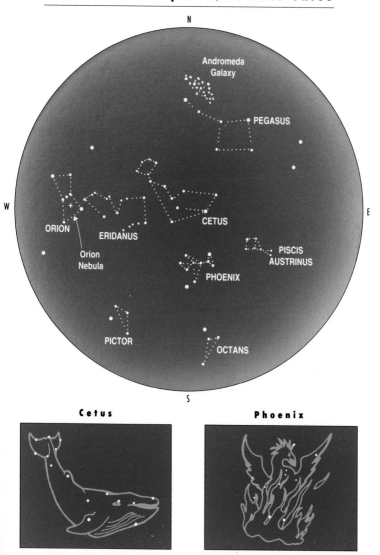

N

Andromeda Galaxy

PEGASUS

ORION

ERIDANUS

Orion Nebula

CETUS

PISCIS AUSTRINUS

PHOENIX

W

E

PICTOR

OCTANS

S

Cetus

Phoenix

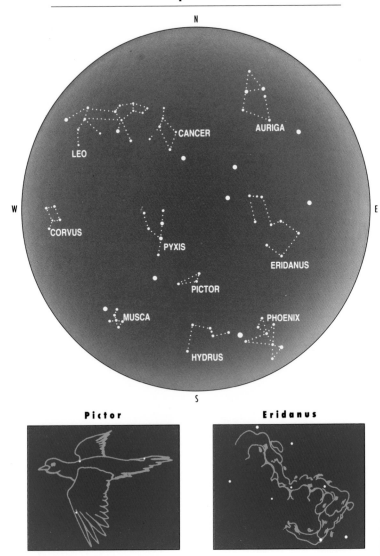

N

W   E

S

LEO

CANCER

AURIGA

CORVUS

PYXIS

ERIDANUS

PICTOR

MUSCA

PHOENIX

HYDRUS

Pictor

Eridanus

Southern Hemisphere/Winter Skies

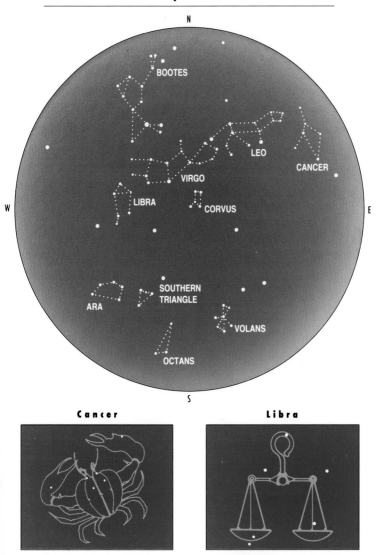

N

BOOTES

LEO

CANCER

VIRGO

LIBRA

CORVUS

SOUTHERN
TRIANGLE

ARA

VOLANS

OCTANS

W

E

S

Cancer

Libra

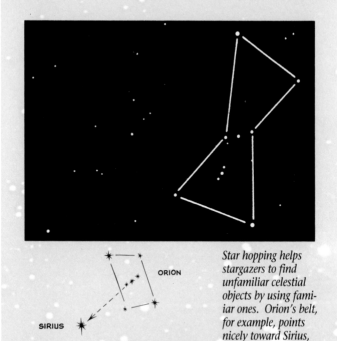

Star hopping helps stargazers to find unfamiliar celestial objects by using familiar ones. Orion's belt, for example, points nicely toward Sirius, the brightest star in the heavens.

westward and you encounter Aldebaran, the brightest star in Taurus, the Bull.

You are not limited to the arrows shown on the star maps. In fact, it is a lot of fun to develop your own star-hopping techniques. Once you do, you may wish to advance to more detailed star maps, which you can find in monthly astronomy periodicals or at the gift shop of your local planetarium or science museum. These maps will show many more stars than those included here and will help to prepare you for using binoculars and telescopes later on.

Stellar Stories

Beginning stargazers often become frustrated because they can't find the picture of a great bear or a flying horse in the sky. That isn't surprising, since the pictures are not really there. The constellations were devised thousands of years ago by wandering peoples who told stories in exchange for food and lodging. These peoples discovered that they could use certain star patterns to represent animals, objects, and heroes in their stories, which were then passed down from generation to generation.

In the Northern Hemisphere, these peoples told stories of Orion, the Mighty Hunter, accompanied by his two trusty hunting dogs, Canis Major and Canis Minor, chasing Taurus, the Bull, across the sky. In autumn they told of the maiden, Andromeda, chained to a rock in the ocean until Perseus, riding Pegasus, his flying horse, came to rescue her. All of these characters, who form the basis of classical mythology, have been permanently enshrined in the sky.

The star groupings, however, don't really look like these people, animals, or objects. You can connect the stars with lines all night and never see a flying horse or a maiden chained to a rock. In fact, the constellations look no more like what they represent than the Eiffel Tower looks like Alexandre Eiffel. Keeping this in mind should make stargazing much less frustrating.

Today, constellations are more than just historical curiosities. They are quite useful for astronomers, though not in the way they were once intended. Now astronomers define the constellations as areas of the sky. They have divided the sky into 88 areas, each with its own size, shape, and name. Every star belongs to one of the constellations, just as every home resides in a city or town.

Creating Our Own Images

If constellations represent such a strange collection of objects, most of which you could never see even if you knew what they looked like, how can you ever hope to make sense out of the nighttime sky? By creating images you can recognize.

The Big Dipper, for example, is not a true constellation but a star grouping that lies within the constellation of Ursa Major, the Great Bear. The Great Square is a group of four stars that lies within the constellation of Pegasus, the Flying Horse.

These are "asterisms," groups of stars that actually look like something. You can create your own asterisms to help you find your way around the night sky. For example, just to the northeast of the bright star Arcturus lies the aforementioned group of stars known as Boötes, the Herdsman. Far more visible to the modern eye, however, is the shape of a kite. In the Southern Hemisphere, Sagittarius, the Archer, can be more easily recognized by several stars that form a pattern of a teapot.

Asterisms are far easier to see than the original representations. What's more, you can change them to suit your own needs. If, for example, you don't see a hunter in the constellation of Orion, perhaps it will appear to you more easily as an hourglass, a bow tie, or a butterfly.

Geometrical shapes are particularly easy to spot among the stars of the night sky. The largest and most famous are the Great Square of Pegasus, the Summer Triangle (made up of the stars Vega, Deneb, and Altair), and the Great Circle (formed by Rigel, Sirius, Procyon, Pollux, Castor, Capella, and Aldebaran). But you can also find smaller and less obvious groupings; for example, the brightest stars within the constellation of Auriga, the Charioteer, actually form a pentagon, and four stars within Lyra, the Harp, form a neat little parallelogram.

But keep in mind that no matter how real these images may seem, they are only illusions caused by the placement of certain stars in three-dimensional space. You could never go to the Big Dipper, for instance, for it just doesn't exist. If you could fly along through space with the ease that you might drive a car across town, you would gradually see the positions of the stars change dramatically. Only by organizing and grouping stars into recognizable shapes can you begin to understand the heavens and find your way around an otherwise confusing maze of stars.

Chapter 3

Personalities of the Stars

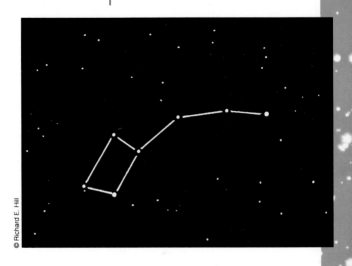

© Richard E. Hill

*"*If you've seen one star, you've seen them all." This is a common cry of beginning stargazers, but it isn't true. Every star in the heavens is as individual as every human on Earth. Like people, you can classify stars into categories and types, but when you really get to know them, their differences shine through magnificently.

Above: The four stars of the Little Dipper's bowl are a useful tool for measuring stellar brightnesses. By comparing other stars with these four, we can estimate their brightnesses.

Naming the Stars

Every star has an official designation. For example, the star HD172167 might also be known to astronomers as SA067174, or even BD+38°3238. The different numbers may be determined by the star's position in the sky, or by its entry in a particular catalog.

Another designation of stars is a Greek letter followed by a latinized constellation name: star HD172167 might also be known as Alpha Lyrae, or the brightest star in Lyra, the Harp. The constellation name indicates the area of the sky in which the star can be found. The Greek letter (i.e., alpha, beta, gamma, delta, epsilon, etc.) signifies the relative brightness of the star within that constellation.

But the best way to get to know stars is to learn their proper names. After all, how many people do you know by their Social Security number, or by the designation "the shortest kid in the Smith family"? Therefore, the star HD172167 is also known as Vega. Vega is a very different star than Antares, and both are different from the sun. Like people, stars possess distinguishing characteristics.

Classifying and Estimating Brightnesses

One of the distinguishing features between stars, of course, is brightness. Some stars are intrinsically brighter than the sun, but most are much fainter. For this reason, you cannot judge a star's distance from its brightness alone. For example, a candle is considerably fainter than a car headlight, but if you move that headlight a mile (1.67km) away, the candle will appear to outshine it. The same is true with stars.

Astronomers measure a star's "apparent" brightness with a numerical scale called "magnitude." Hipparchus, an ancient Greek astronomer, first developed this measurement scheme. He divided the sky into six categories. He classified the brightest stars as 1st magnitude. The next brightest were 2nd magnitude; these appeared about 2.5 times fainter than 1st magnitude. Third, 4th, and 5th magnitude followed, each about 2.5 times fainter than the magnitude before it.

In other words, a 5th-magnitude star appears about 2.5 times fainter than a 4th-magnitude star, about 6.25 (2.5 × 2.5) times fainter than a 3rd-magnitude star, about 15.63 (2.5 × 2.5 × 2.5) times fainter than a 2nd-magnitude star, and so on. Hipparchus classified the faintest stars visible to the naked eye as 6th magnitude, which appear about 100 times (2.5 × 2.5 × 2.5 × 2.5 × 2.5) fainter than a 1st-magnitude star.

As far as Hipparchus could tell, there were no stars fainter than 6th magnitude. But when astronomers turned their telescopes toward the heavens in the seventeenth century, they found that there were more stars that were fainter than 6th magnitude than brighter. Consequently, astronomers began to expand the magnitude scale. Those stars just beyond the visibility of the human eye were called 7th magnitude, then 8th, 9th, and so on. Today, the largest and most powerful telescopes in the world can see stars as faint as 25th magnitude, or 39 million times (2.5 times itself 19 times) fainter than those visible to the unaided eye.

In addition, when astronomers began to look in detail at the measurement system, they discovered that Hipparchus had lumped together in the 1st-magnitude category objects as different in brightness as the star Sirius, the moon, and the sun. For this reason, astronomers expanded the magnitude scale in the opposite direction as well. Stars 2.5 times brighter than 1st magnitude became 0 magnitude; those 2.5 times brighter still became −1 magnitude, and so on. (The moon, by the way, works out to be about −12.7 magnitude. The sun shines at a remarkable −26.7 magnitude.)

Today, stellar brightnesses are measured with electronic detectors called photometers, but, with practice, they can be estimated by eye. The trick is to compare an unknown star brightness with a known one. Northern

Hemisphere observers have a wonderful beginning guide to measuring stellar magnitudes within the bowl of the Little Dipper.

The Little Dipper can always be located, since the end of its handle is marked by Polaris, the North Star. The Little Dipper appears smaller, upside down, and fainter than its bigger counterpart, the Big Dipper. Nevertheless, the Little Dipper's bowl contains four stars, each of a different magnitude: 2nd, 3rd, 4th, and 5th. The bowl provides a basis for comparison of other stars' brightnesses. In addition, since the entire Little Dipper is often obscured by bright city lights or moonlight, it also provides a method of gauging the quality of the sky.

If you can see only the brightest star in the Little Dipper's bowl, for example, this means you cannot see fainter than 2nd magnitude. This would not be a good night to search for faint constellations such as Cancer, the Crab, or Delphinus, the Dolphin. If, on the other hand, you can see three or four of the Little Dipper's bowl stars with the naked eye, that means your visibility limit is 4th or 5th magnitude, so you should be able to see stars down to that brightness.

Although Southern Hemisphere observers don't have a constellation that is directly comparable to the Little Dipper in terms of its easily identifiable shape, they can look to the constellation of Carina to find stars of the same magnitude. Although it is not easy to describe how to locate them, there are four stars within the Carina constellation that have the same magnitudes as those of the Little Dipper.

Colorful Stars

Stars come not only in a variety of brightnesses, but a variety of colors as well. Unlike brightness, however, which depends both on a star's intrinsic luminosity as well as its distance, color depends only on a star's temperature. As regards color, a star works much the same as molten steel or glass when either one is heated; it may

RED GIANT

Stars come in all sizes and colors. They range in size from red giants, many times larger than our sun, to white dwarfs, smaller than Earth.

ALPHA CENTURI TAR SYSTEM

ORANGE STAR

WHITE DWARF

YELLOW STAR

WHITE STAR

BLUE GIANT

appear "red hot" at first, but as its temperature rises, its color changes to orange, yellow, white, and, finally, blue.

Many stars, like the sun, are simply white stars: their gases shine at a temperature of some 10,000°F (5,500°C). Cooler stars—those with temperatures of 5,000 to 6,000°F (2,700 to 3,300°C)—appear to our eyes as reddish or orange. Those stars as hot as 20,000 to 30,000°F (11,000 to 17,000°C) may appear bluish white.

Since our color perception depends on the color receptors in our eyes, and since these receptors work only when there is plenty of light, we see color in only the brightest of stars. Even when we do see such color, it is subtle, and may be missed entirely by an observer with some color blindness.

Double Stars

Not all stars are single. In fact, the more you gaze around the sky, the more you will see stars that appear double. Many "double stars" are simply an optical illusion, caused by two stars appearing along nearly the same line of sight.

One of the most famous double stars is located in the Northern Hemisphere star grouping known as the Big Dipper, at the curve of its handle. Here are the stars Alcor and Mizar, often dubbed the "Horse and Rider." The ancient Arabs called this pair of stars the "proof," for if someone could see its two stars it was proof that he had good eyesight—and he was then inducted into the army!

Other double stars are not quite so easy to spot. Epsilon Lyrae, for example, the faint star just to the east of the brilliant summer star Vega in Lyra, the Harp, is also a double. But only terrific eyesight, coupled with excellent sky transparency and seeing, makes this pair visible.

Variable Stars

Not all stars appear the same brightness all the time. Even a star as notable as the North Star is a well-known "variable star." Variable stars may change in brightness just slightly or by quite a bit. Some, like Delta Cephei, actually change their brightness from about 3.5 magni-

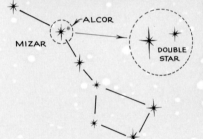

One of the most famous of all double stars visible to the naked eye can be found in the handle of the Big Dipper. A small telescope shows Mizar to be part of a binary star.

tude to 4.4 magnitude in a little over five days. This star does so because it is actually swelling and contracting.

Other variable stars change their brightnesses over a period of nearly a year. Omicron Ceti, also known as Mira the Wonderful, goes from being one of the brightest stars (magnitude 2.0) in our sky to invisibility (magnitude 10.1) in 332 days. That means that, at times, this star may appear on your star map, but not in the sky. Some variable stars change in apparent brightness because of instabilities within their atmospheres.

A star also may change in brightness because another star—one in orbit around it—passes in front of it and temporarily blocks it from view. Such stars are called "eclipsing binary stars." One of the most famous eclipsing binaries is known as Algol, the Demon Star, or Beta Persei; this star changes in brightness from magnitude 2.1 to 3.3 in just three days.

It is also interesting to note that variable stars are named differently from normal stars. For example, when a variable star is discovered in a constellation, say Sagittarius, it is designated R Sagittarii. The second one to be found there is named S Sagittarii, the third T Sagittarii, and so on. When Z Sagittarii is reached, the letter prefix becomes double, beginning with RR. This designation continues RS, RT, RU...and so on. Eventually ZZ Sagittarii is reached, and the letters revert back to the beginning of the alphabet: AA, AB, AC...and so on up to QQ Sagittarii. The single letters A through Q are not used, since they had been used previously to name newly discovered stars in the Southern Hemisphere sky.

By this method, 334 variable stars can be designated in any one constellation. Instead of continuing with triple-letter combinations, astronomers continue with V335, V336, V337, etc. In this way, an infinity of variable stars can be numbered. And how many are there? More than 1,135 have been cataloged in Sagittarius alone.

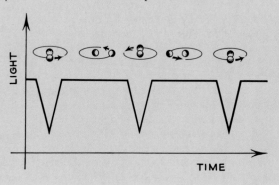

Some binary stars orbit in a plane perpendicular to our line of sight. We can then see their combined light output change regularly as the two stars orbit and eclipse each other.

Chapter 4

A World in Motion

© FPG International

The world on which we live is a planet nearly 8,000 miles (12,800km) in diameter. Though we've known this fact for thousands of years, it's not at all obvious to stargazers looking into the night sky. In fact, to a stargazer our world appears quite flat and motionless. Of course, this is not true: our world is one of nine separate planets spinning their way through space and actually moves in several different directions at once.

Above: Our world is the spaceship on which we are carried across the universe. It contains all the air, food, and water that living things need to survive.

Our world completes one full rotation on its axis every 24 hours. That means that a point on the equator must whirl at nearly 1,100 miles (1,760km) per hour to cover a distance of 26,000 miles (41,600km) every 24 hours. The ancients considered this, of course, but discounted the idea, for if it were true, then everything would be blown off the world by the tremendous gales. The ancients never considered that the air might be moving with us at the same speed.

The Earth, we also know today, orbits the sun in about 365¼ days, the period we use to define a year. As the Earth lies at an average distance of 93 million miles (148,800,000km) from the sun, it must travel some 584 million miles (934,400,000km) in this period. In other words, we on Earth are whipping along at 67,000 miles (107,200km) per hour!

Daily Motion

If we are moving so quickly, why then doesn't the sky change rapidly as we fly through space? The fact is, it does. You can watch the daily rotation of the Earth quite easily. Everyone has done so while watching the sun rise in the east or set in the west. Not only does the sun appear to move in this way, so do the moon, planets, and stars. They all appear to rise in the east and set in the west.

Actually, it is incorrect to speak of the moon, planets, and stars as "rising" or "setting," since this implies that they are moving around us. It is more correct to say that the eastern horizon of Earth is constantly "dropping" and uncovering new objects, while the western horizon is "rising" upward and covering others.

To watch this effect is very simple. Northern Hemisphere stargazers should choose a prominent star or constellation in the southern part of the sky just after dark. Those observers south of the equator should pick one in the northern part of the sky. Note its exact position relative to a nearby landmark, such as a tree, a telephone pole, or a chimney. Go out to the same spot an hour later and note its new position.

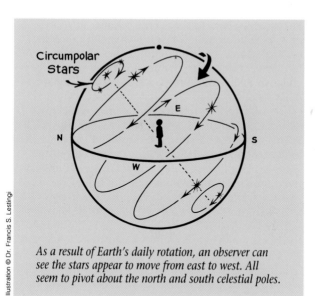

As a result of Earth's daily rotation, an observer can see the stars appear to move from east to west. All seem to pivot about the north and south celestial poles.

If you were careful in your measurement, you may have noticed that the object changed its position westward across the sky. If you measured its position with your little finger or fist held at arm's length, you may have discovered that the object moved at a rate of about 15 degrees westward every hour. If you were particularly patient, you may have discovered that the star was moving at a speed of 1 degree every 4 minutes—or about the width of your outstretched little finger every 2 minutes!

For Northern Hemisphere observers, this method works well with stars in the eastern, southern, or western sky. Similarly, for those in the Southern Hemisphere, this works best with stars in the east, north, or west.

If you watch the stars in the sky opposite the celestial pole, they all will appear to move steadily across the sky from east to west in nearly straight lines. They will rise in the east, move across our sky, and set in the west.

But those in the direction of the celestial poles seem only to circle around in much smaller circles. All are centered about the point defining the celestial pole. In fact, some stars don't even rise or set, but just wheel endlessly about this point. Such stars are called circumpolar stars.

Finally, the star that moves the least—actually, it hardly moves at all—is Polaris. This is due to the fact that Polaris stands directly over the North Pole. Polaris' lack of movement is a very handy feature of the night sky for Northern Hemisphere observers, and it is a feature that is not duplicated in the Southern Hemisphere. This means that if you stood at the North Pole, you would see Polaris at the zenith. In other words, Polaris' altitude above the horizon would be 90 degrees—the same as the latitude of the North Pole. Here, every star would appear circumpolar, since none would ever rise or set.

If you walked southward on the globe, what you would see in the sky would change. Polaris would appear to drop lower and lower in the northern sky, and by the time you got to the Earth's equator, the star would appear directly on the northern horizon. Polaris' altitude above the northern horizon—0 degrees—would remain equal to the latitude. From here, no star would be circumpolar, since all would rise in the east and set in the west.

By measuring the altitude of the North Star you can easily estimate your latitude, no matter where you are in the Earth's Northern Hemisphere. For example, someone in San Diego would see Polaris 32 degrees above the northern horizon.

Annual Motion

A second type of sky motion, annual motion, requires more patience to see. Annual motion is caused by the Earth's annual swing around the sun.

If you could see the sun and stars in the daytime, you would be able to see the sun appear to drift eastward through the stars each day. Since the Earth revolves around the sun (360 degrees) every 365 days, the sun would appear to change its position by about 1 degree in the opposite direction each day.

While we can't see the motion of the sun directly, we can see the results of its motion in the night sky. To do so, select a prominent star or constellation low in the eastern sky and observe it at the same time on a clear evening for the next few weeks.

What you'll find is that the star seems to shift slowly westward over time; this is due to the fact that we are orbiting the sun and looking at the nighttime sky from a slightly different point each night. You'll notice that the star you've chosen seems to lie 1 degree farther west at the same time each evening. This also means that the star should reach the same point 4 minutes earlier each evening.

At 7 P.M. on March 1, for example, your star might appear exactly on the eastern horizon. The next night it should appear there at 6:56, the night after that at 6:52,

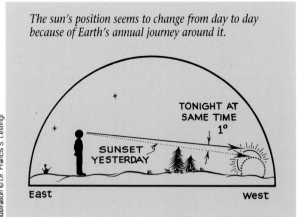

The sun's position seems to change from day to day because of Earth's annual journey around it.

and so on. By the end of 1 month, the star will lie at that point 2 hours earlier; in 2 months, 4 hours earlier. By March 1 of the next year, that same star will appear once again at the same point on the eastern horizon at exactly 7 P.M.

So while the nighttime sky changes by only 1 degree per night, over time that change accumulates and produces the "seasonal" skies that we see. This is why it is necessary to use different star maps for different seasons of the year.

Nevertheless, whatever else changes in the sky, the stars near the celestial poles shine during spring and summer, autumn and winter, circling in an everlasting ballet.

Chapter 5

Is the Moon Up Tonight?

© W. Perry Conway/Tom Stack & Associates

The moon is our natural satellite. Nearly a quarter of a million miles (384,500km) from the Earth, it orbits our planet once every month and, as a result, never stays in one place very long.

You can see how the moon moves by noting its exact position in the sky relative to a landmark such as a tree or telephone pole. The next night, observe the moon from the same place at the same time: the moon will appear farther to the east. If you observe

Above: The moon always seems larger when it rises or sets over the horizon. As real as this appears, the effect is caused by an optical trick known as "the moon illusion."

As the moon orbits the Earth from west to east, we can see its position against the background stars change from night to night.

the moon in this way for several nights, its motion will become quite clear.

Since the moon orbits our Earth from west to east nearly every 29.5 days, it must move about approximately 12 degrees eastward each day. From this knowledge, you can easily predict its position from night to night. Simply use your fist to measure out 12 degrees east of the moon's current position and note it on your star map. The next night, check your prediction to see how close you were; with practice, it will become easier to be more accurate.

While moving 12 degrees per day may not sound very fast, it means that the moon must move eastward through the stars with a speed of half a degree—or one full moon-diameter—every hour. In other words, the moon's movement is actually relatively fast—and easy to see.

To do so, accurately sketch the moon's position relative to some nearby stars on your star map. About an hour later, go outdoors and sketch the moon's position relative to the same stars. If you were careful in your observations, you will have seen the moon change its position against those stars by one full diameter.

The Moon's Changing Shape: Lunar Phases

As the moon drifts eastward on its monthly journey around the Earth, it also seems to change shape. The ancient Greeks had figured out these lunar "phases"; they understood that as the moon moved around our planet, it was illuminated from different angles by the sun— hence its solid and spherical shapes. This is also why we on Earth see a differently shaped moon each night.

When the moon appears in the direction of the sun, it is illuminated from the back—only the dark side faces us. This, coupled with the fact that the moon lies very near the sun in our sky, makes it impossible to see. The moon in this phase is called a "new moon," because it defines the beginning of a new lunar cycle. The new moon does everything the sun does—it rises and sets at about the same time, and moves across the sky in the same path.

As the moon moves eastward though the stars, it continues to "grow." Now the moon appears in the western sky at sunset, its side illuminated by the sun. At this point, the moon is called a "waxing" crescent moon. Anyone viewing the moon during this time is bound to see its full disk faintly illuminated under a bright crescent. This phenomenon, which is caused by sunlight reflecting back to the moon off the Earth, is called "earthshine."

As you view the waxing crescent moon, keep in mind that someone looking back from the moon would see a nearly full Earth in their sky. Just as a full moon illuminates our nighttime landscape here on Earth, a full Earth illuminates the dark landscape of the moon.

Seven days after new moon, the moon lies 90 degrees east of the sun, and appears due south at sunset for observers in the Northern Hemisphere, and due

Earthshine is caused by sunlight being reflected back to the dark side of the moon by the Earth itself.

north for those in the Southern Hemisphere. This lunar phase is called "first quarter" because one quarter of the moon's surface is now visible. If you look in the eastern sky in the late afternoon, you usually can see a first-quarter moon in full daylight.

As the moon continues its eastward motion around the Earth, it grows in size until it appears as a more rounded shape—a "gibbous" phase—and farther from the sun in our sky. This phenomenon can be seen in the late afternoon, before the sun goes down completely.

About two weeks after new moon, the full moon

As the moon orbits our Earth, it "waxes" from crescent to quarter to gibbous to full.

occurs. At this point, the full face of the moon is lit by the sun. The full moon always lies opposite the sun in our sky, and moves in opposition to the sun. A true full moon is the only lunar phase that can never be seen when the sun is in the sky.

The full moon rises in the east, just as the sun sets in the west. If you observe the moon as it rises above the horizon, then again a few hours later, it will appear much smaller. But the moon's size has not really changed at all. You've simply experienced one of nature's oldest optical illusions: the moon illusion.

To prove to yourself that the large moon is only an illusion, make a loose fist with your hand and, keeping one eye shut, look at the rising moon through it. The moon will appear to shrink in size. Now blink back and forth between your two eyes—the one looking straight at the moon and the one looking through your fist—and the moon will appear to swell and shrink.

No one knows for certain what causes the moon illusion, but some scientists think that the foreground land objects actually fool your eyes into believing the moon is larger than it really is. By looking through a loose fist, you eliminate the foreground objects from view, and you see a normal-sized moon once again.

As the moon continues its eastward motion around the Earth, it is now in a "waning" gibbous phase, rising

The moon also "wanes" from (almost) full to gibbous to quarter to crescent.

© Lick Observatory

later and later after sunset and seldom seen by those who retire to their homes before midnight.

Seven days after full moon, the moon lies at right angles to the sun again, but this time on the opposite side of the sky. Now the moon rises around midnight and lies due south at sunrise for those in the Northern Hemisphere, and due north for those below the equator. This is a moon that is often visible in the early morning sky to casual sky watchers, and is known as a "last quarter" moon.

The moon's shape continues to shrink, as it once again approaches the sun. The waning crescent moon is visible only to those who rise before the sun. Now the crescent lies low in the east before dawn, its eastern side illuminated by the sun.

The cycle is now complete. The moon lies between the sun and Earth once again, and the cycle begins anew.

The Man in the Moon

Most of us have noticed the moon's light and dark shadings, which produce that illusory face often referred to as the "man in the moon." Some of us have even seen objects other than a man's face— a lady with a sparkling diamond necklace, a frog, and even Bugs Bunny.

Ancient sky watchers had a variety of explanations for the moon. Some believed it to be a goddess. Others believed it was a giant mirror in which the image of our own world was reflected. Still others believed the moon's dark shadings were oceans of water, making it a world just like the Earth, complete with living beings.

These theories, of course, came long before the invention of the telescope. Today, we know that the dark patches we see from Earth are dry plains of solidified lava, left over from the moon's early days. Even though there is not a drop of water on this barren, rocky world, the dark areas are still known as "maria," or seas: the Sea of Tranquility, the Sea of Vapors, the Sea of Foam, and the Sea of Serenity, among others.

What is most remarkable is that, as the moon goes

Chapter 6

The Wandering Stars

Our Earth is part of a family of worlds known as the solar system—nine planets, dozens of moons, countless asteroids, meteoroids, and comets, all whirling about the sun. Those closest to the sun move the fastest and require the least time to complete one orbit. Mercury, for example—only 36 million miles (57.6 million km) away from the sun—takes 88 Earth days to complete one revo-

Above: Planets often look just like bright stars in the sky. Venus and Mercury, however, can only be seen shortly after sunset or just before sunrise.

lution, while Pluto—more than 3 billion miles (4.8 billion km) away—requires nearly two and a half centuries to orbit once.

Seeing Planets

It is not uncommon to see five different planets in the sky in one evening, for Mercury, Venus, Mars, Jupiter, and Saturn shine brightly nearly all the time. Simply go outdoors on any clear night, look up, and chances are that at least one is within your view.

Several tricks exist to distinguish planets from stars. For one, planets are often brighter than stars. While planets are physically much smaller than stars and shine only because they reflect sunlight, they are much closer and therefore shine more brightly in our sky.

A second technique for identifying a planet is to look along a well-defined band of constellations known as the zodiac. Planets can be found here since they orbit the sun in a plane. Since we are inside that plane, the planets appear to lie along a thin band stretching across the sky. The constellations behind them are those of the zodiac. From the Earth's Northern Hemisphere these constellations may appear in the east, south, or west. From the Southern Hemisphere, they may appear in the east, west, or north.

A third way of spotting a planet is to notice if it is twinkling. Planets generally don't appear to twinkle as stars do. Because they are closer to us than stars, they actually appear in our sky as disks. While we cannot easily distinguish their disks with the unaided eye, it is their disks that often keep them from twinkling. Their light is bounced around as much as starlight is, but because that light comes from a disk rather than a point source, planets' twinkling is not as noticeable as stars'. Only on nights of extremely bad seeing, or when a planet shines very low in the sky, will planets appear to twinkle noticeably.

Finally, the very best and most definitive method for determining if an object is a planet is by watching its motion. Planets orbit the sun and, from our perspective on the Earth within that plane of motion, we can see them moving about through the more distant stars.

It was the ancient stargazers who first noticed the planets' motion, though they had no idea what caused it. In fact, the very name "planets" comes from the Greek word *planetes* meaning "wanderers." If you watch the skies over several days or weeks, you too will see their wanderings.

Planets seem to move through the stars as they orbit the sun. Notice the eastward movement of Jupiter (brightest object) relative to the stars of the teapot of Sagittarius.

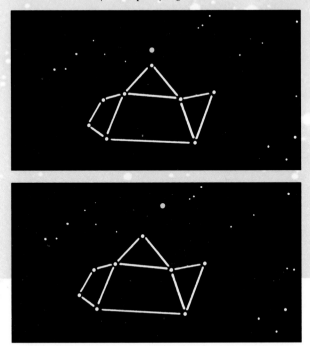

You can track the motion of a planet (or planet candidate) by noting its position and carefully plotting that position relative to the nearby stars. Every few nights, go outdoors and carefully check the planet's position relative to those same stars. If what you're tracking is indeed a planet, chances are you'll see its motion within a week or so.

Of the five planets visible from your backyard, two lie closer to the sun than the Earth. Venus is the brightest of all, while Mercury can be very faint and difficult to see. Because these worlds orbit closest to the sun, they always lie near the sun in our sky. They can be seen only shortly after sunset or just before sunrise. Because of its dazzling brilliance, Venus is often mistaken for an airplane with landing lights and sometimes even a UFO.

If you watch these planets regularly at sunset, you will notice them drifting farther eastward from the sun over time. Then, days or weeks later, they will turn and head westward until they are lost in its glare once again. As they orbit past the sun, they will emerge on its western side. In a few weeks, they will set before the sun and be visible only in the eastern sky before sunrise.

The remaining three planets visible to the naked eye—Mars, Jupiter, and Saturn—cannot compare to the brilliance of Venus. They lie farther from and take noticeably longer to orbit the sun than does Earth; Mars takes nearly two Earth years to make its orbit, Jupiter takes about twelve; and Saturn almost three decades.

These planets can appear farther from the sun in our sky than either Venus or Mercury and, as a result, their motions are not so simple. Often these planets drift eastward through the starry sky; this is called "direct" motion. But occasionally, they will appear to stop their eastward motion, turn around, and head westward for a few weeks or so; this is referred to as "retrograde" motion. Eventually, they will stop their westward motion and head eastward once again.

Retrograde motion occurs only when a planet lies at "opposition"—the place in the sky opposite the sun. In other words, if you see Mars low in the eastern sky at

UFOs

Occasionally people see objects or phenomena in the sky that they cannot explain. These objects are often dubbed "unidentified flying objects," or UFOs.

In our modern culture, UFOs are often associated with flying craft from other worlds. But since zipping around the cosmos in spacecraft is virtually impossible, scientists prefer to think of UFOs as just what their name states: unidentified flying objects.

Most objects that are seen in the sky, no matter how strange they appear, actually can be identified by someone who knows the sky. That's why people who generally see UFOs are those who seldom look upward. In other words, what they see startles them since they don't understand it.

Any object that cannot be identified can be classified as a UFO: the moon, a cloud, a meteor, an Earth-orbiting satellite, a weather balloon or dirigible, or other bizarre lights in the sky. At some time, everyone will see a UFO. There's no need to panic; just record everything about the object that you possibly can:

- Date and time
- Where you are
- Conditions of the sky
- Position of the object (altitude and azimuth)
- Speed of the object (degrees per second)
- Direction of motion
- Color
- Brightness
- Take a photograph or video

If you record as many features of the object as possible, as well as any other condition that may affect your vision, you can assist authorities in changing the UFO to an IFO—an identified flying object.

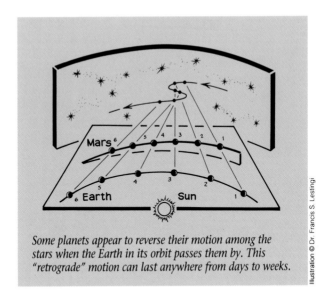

Some planets appear to reverse their motion among the stars when the Earth in its orbit passes them by. This "retrograde" motion can last anywhere from days to weeks.

sunset, you can expect it to be undergoing a retrograde loop over the next few weeks.

While these loops may seem terribly confusing at first, their cause is really quite simple. They occur as our world speeds past the planet and causes it to move backward temporarily against the more distant background stars, just as a car appears to go backward as we pass it on the highway.

Occasionally, during their endless dance through the stars, two or more planets may appear in the same part of the sky. Of course, the planets really aren't near each other, and there's no danger of a collision. They just appear for a time to lie along nearly the same line of sight. This is called a "conjunction."

When brilliant Jupiter and Venus appear together against the glow of dawn or dusk, the effect can be remarkably beautiful. When the moon passes by that area, particularly if it passes by against a sunset or sunrise, it can create a most memorable sight.

Zodiacal Lights

Planets are not the only members of our solar system visible to the naked eye, for scattered between the planets is a tremendous amount of debris left over from the birth of our planetary family 5 billion years ago.

On a moonless night in spring in the Northern Hemisphere, look for a hazy triangular band stretching upward from the western horizon immediately after dark. In autumn, you can see this band in the eastern sky before dawn; its base lies near the horizon and it rises upward into the constellations of the zodiac. In its brightest parts, it exceeds the brilliance of the Milky Way. This band is called the zodiacal light.

Another phenomenon to search for—and one that is far more difficult to see—is known as the *gegenschein*, or "counterglow." During the months of September to November, counterglow appears in the constellation of Pisces, the Fish, while during January and February, it

At times, a number of solar system objects can appear in the same area of the sky, creating spectacular groupings for viewing or photography. This photo shows the moon, Venus, and Jupiter.

lies within Cancer, the Crab. Around midnight during that time, look high overhead for a faint, somewhat elliptical glow about 10 degrees in width.

These glows are caused by sunlight being scattered by dust particles in our solar system. They are extremely faint, so if there is any haze, moonlight, or light pollution, you may never see them.

Comets

Comets are chunks of ice and rock that orbit the sun in the depths of our solar system—far beyond the orbit of Pluto. Occasionally, however, the gravity of the sun tugs a comet inward, forcing it to swing in past the Earth; as it does, the sun's light and heat vaporize its ices, and the solar wind blows the cometary material outward into what we see as a long and beautiful tail.

Usually half a dozen or so new comets are discovered each year. Most are found by backyard comet hunters, and are named after their discoverers, but only the very nearest and brightest can be seen by naked-eye observers. Some comets, like Comet Ikeya-Seki (1965) are dazzling, their brilliant tails stretching completely across the sky. Others, like Comet Kohoutek (1973), are a disappointment, as they are barely visible.

A bright comet, drifting majestically from night to night among the stars, is one the most magnificent sights in nature. Perhaps the most famous of all comets is Halley's, which orbits the sun every seventy-six years. During its last visit in 1986, Halley's Comet was not very bright, for it never came that close to Earth.

Meteors

When observing the sky, a star may occasionally appear to flash suddenly in front of you. Actually, such "shooting" or "falling" stars have nothing to do with stars at all, except that they look like one dropping from above. What most people call falling stars are technically known as meteors.

Meteors are simply specks of dust smaller than a grain of sand that fall into our upper atmosphere from

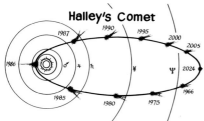

Halley's Comet

Halley's Comet, the most famous of all comets, orbits the sun once every seventy-six years. As it approaches the sun, its tail grows and brightens enough to become visible from Earth.

space. As meteors encounter the air, the friction heats them up until they vaporize in a flash.

While tumbling through space, these particles are known as "meteoroids." As a meteoroid plunges into the atmosphere and burns up, it is referred to as a "meteor." Finally, if a meteor is large enough to survive its fiery plunge to Earth and hit the ground, it is then known as a "meteorite." Fortunately for living things, such large chunks of stone and iron are few and far between.

Even the very smallest of meteors can appear quite spectacular in the sky. Some fall very quickly, while others barely seem to move. Their colors may range over the entire spectrum: white, orange, red, blue, and green. Some of the more spectacular meteors might leave behind smoke trails, or even cast a shadow; these are called "fireballs." Others, known as "bolides," may whistle, sizzle, or even create a sonic boom as they fall.

If you go outdoors on any clear, dark night, you're

bound to see several meteors falling from the sky every hour. These are called "sporadic" meteors, and there is no way of knowing when or where they will appear. There is, however, a method of improving your chances of seeing meteors: watching a meteor shower.

As the Earth moves in its orbit around the sun, it occasionally encounters swarms of these meteoric particles, most of which have been left along the orbits of ancient comets. As the Earth plows forward into these particles, an observer on the ground might see as many as one or two meteors falling from the sky every minute. These meteors all seem to come from one general direction in the sky, and that direction is called the "radiant" of the shower. The radiant is named for the constellation that appears behind it: Leonids, Orionids, Geminids, among others.

Several meteor showers occur each year. To view one, watch the skies after midnight, for this is the time when we are facing in the direction of the Earth's motion through space. Just as the front windshield of a car gets pelted harder by falling rain than the rear window, early morning observers are looking out the "front window" of Earth, and therefore can often see more meteors falling inward.

To watch a shower, all you need is a reclining lounge chair and a blanket or a warm sleeping bag. You might want to sketch each meteor you see on your star map. Every meteor that originates from the swarm will seem to come from the radiant.

The most famous and reliable shower is known as the Perseids, named for the constellation Perseus. This shower occurs every year in mid-August and, on a good clear, dark night, Perseid watchers can often see four or five dozen meteors falling from the sky every hour.

Opposite page: During meteor showers, specks of glowing dust appear to rain out of the sky. Inset: Every few million years, a huge chunk of iron might fall and blast a crater like this one in northern Arizona.

Principal Meteor Showers

Date of Maximum*	Shower Name	Best Hour to Watch	Hourly Rate**	Associated Comet
January 4	Quadrantids	5 A.M.	40–150	—
April 21	Lyrids	4 A.M.	10–15	1861 I
May 4	Eta Aquarids	4 A.M.	10–40	Halley
July 30	Delta Aquarids	2 A.M.	10–35	—
August 11–13	Perseids	4 A.M.	50–100	1862 III
October 9	Draconids	9 P.M.	10	Giacobini-Zinner
October 20	Orionids	4 A.M.	10–70	Halley
November 9	Taurids	Midnight	5–15	Encke
November 16	Leonids	5 A.M.	5–20	1866 I
November 25–27	Andromedids	10 P.M.	10	Biela
December 13	Geminids	2 A.M.	50–80	—
December 22	Ursids	5 A.M.	10–15	—

*Date of actual maximum occurrence may vary by one or two days in either direction.
**Hourly rate refers to the number of meteors you can expect to see per hour. The hourly rate varies from year to year.

Chapter 7

Photographing
the Sky

© Dennis Mammana

You can record anything you can see in the night sky on photographic film. In fact, because of the techniques used in astrophotography, even objects invisible to the eye may show up in photography; this can be either a good or bad surprise, depending, of course, on what you are trying to accomplish in the first place.

Above: This photograph of Halley's Comet was taken with a 35mm camera, a 50mm lens, and 400 ISO color film.

Equipment

To photograph the wonders of the night sky, you need only the simplest of photographic equipment. The first and most obvious is a camera. Any camera will do, but a 35mm camera might be preferable, since you can take long-time-exposure photographs with it. Long-time exposures are necessary since light from the night sky is very faint.

Secondly, the type of lens you use is very important. Most 35mm cameras come with a normal 50mm lens. This number represents the focal length of the lens, that is, the distance from the lens itself to the film plane. Longer focal-length lenses (e.g., 135mm, 200mm, 400mm) produce higher magnification and cover a very small field of view. While this may be beneficial for some types of photography, most sky photography is best done with a normal or wide-angle lens.

The third component of your setup, the tripod, will be responsible for holding your camera steady. A solid

The most useful type of camera for sky photography is one in which lenses can be switched from wide-angle to telephoto.

tripod is necessary whenever time exposures are taken. To help prevent vibrations, use a cable release to trigger the shutter.

As for film, the type you use is really a matter of personal preference, but it should have a relatively high speed. This is indicated by its ASA or ISO rating. For example, 100 speed film is average; a film rated at 200 speed is twice as fast, meaning that it can record the same image in half the time.

Unfortunately, the faster the film you use, the grainier your final pictures will be. This is undesirable if you want to make the photographs into enlargements. It is up to you to pick the film that is appropriate for each application.

Whether you use slide or print film is also a matter of personal preference. Slide film is a good choice if you wish to see the exact piece of celluloid that passed through the camera, or if you need to show your images to groups. Prints are a good choice if you want to be able to "correct" or adjust your images in the lab later. If you are going to shoot a lot of film, you may decide to use slides, as they are less expensive to process. Slides also can be turned into very nice prints if you so desire.

Most celestial sights appear to the eye to be relatively colorless, but not so to the camera. Film records light and color differently than the human eye, so stars that appear as white to our eyes may appear on film as a variety of colors from red to yellow to blue. Color film is always a wise choice when shooting the sky.

The Secret of Good Sky Photography

Light coming from the sky is very faint, and you cannot rely on light meters to tell you proper exposures. Sky fog, moonlight, and light pollution can all affect the appearance of sky photographs—sometimes for better, sometimes for worse.

The secret to producing one great sky photograph is to take twenty and throw nineteen away. This is because there is no accurate way to judge the final results before-hand. The term photographers use for this is "bracket-ing." Bracketing means taking a number of different photographs of the same object, while slightly altering the exposure or aperture as you do. Doing so may pro-duce a number of bad pictures, but within the group there may also be one or two good ones. Sometimes bracketing will produce a terrific picture that you never really expected. Since film is relatively inexpensive com-pared to missing a photographic opportunity, bracketing generously is always a good idea.

Additionally, since most sky photography consists of trial and error, it is extremely important to record as much data as possible about your photographs. Keeping records will help you to learn what works and to select photographs for reprinting.

Information for your logbook should include the date, time, and location of the object photographed; the camera, lens, aperture setting, film type, and speed you used; your exposure times; the sky conditions; the posi-tion and phase of the moon; and processing information. It's also a good idea to record any other data that you feel will help you reshoot your photographs if necessary.

Taking Photographs

Beginning sky photographers may want to start record-ing the night sky on film by taking pictures of a bright constellation, as bright constellations are some of the easiest sky photographs to take. Begin with 200 or 400 speed color film. Set up your camera on a tripod, aim it upward toward a familiar group of stars, and focus it on infinity (∞). Open the lens as wide as possible and take several exposures of the sky: 2 seconds, 4, 8, 15, 30..., doubling the length of each successive exposure. You'll probably take your best at a 15-second exposure. If you've used a 50mm lens on your camera, these pho-tographs will show every star visible to the naked eye, and will record colors you didn't see at the time.

With this technique, it is very easy to record every

depends on your lens and film speed. For 100-speed film, your exposure would be about 1/125 second at f/11. A quarter moon requires about four times the exposure (about 1/125 second at f/5.6), and a thin crescent needs about ten times the light needed to shoot the full moon (about 1/125 at f/2.8). Again, bracketing is wise.

Sunrises and Sunsets

Sunrises and sunsets can produce the most dramatic sky photographs, but in order to take great sunrise and sunset pictures, it's important to keep several things in mind. First, it is extremely dangerous to look at the sun—even the dimmer, reddened setting sun—especially through a camera. Secondly, since the sun and moon appear to be the same size in our sky, they will appear to be the same size on the film as well. If you wish to show a larger sun in your sunset pictures, you will need to use a telephoto lens.

If your camera has a light meter, you can easily

A distorted setting sun was captured with a telephoto lens. By underexposing slightly, you can make the reds and oranges of sunset more dramatic.

© Dennis Milon

determine a starting exposure for a sunset photograph. Simply aim the camera at the sky near the sun (not at it) and get a light reading. Then carefully compose your shot without looking at the setting sun directly. Bracket your exposures so that you underexpose all of your images; if you do, your pictures will show a richer, more colorful sunset than you actually saw.

Processing the Film

Once your film is exposed, process it immediately. If you don't process it right away, keep it in the refrigerator until you do. Since you have been shooting mostly night-time scenes, you will have produced a strip of film that appears to the unsuspecting eye to have absolutely nothing on it. Whether you shoot slides or prints, always provide special instructions to the lab that processes them.

With slides, always request that they be returned uncut and unmounted; if they aren't, they may get sliced right down the middle of each frame, as the automatic cutting machines cannot tell the frame lines apart from the dark sky. Having your slides developed this way will also help you read the frame numbers on each image so that you can compare them with the entries in your logbook.

Secondly, always request that cardboard slide mounts be packaged separately from the slides. This way you can assemble the slides yourself when you decide on the best exposures. Most slide mounts can be sealed with the heat and pressure of a household iron, but be careful not to warp or burn the film inside!

If you are working with negatives, always request that the lab print every frame *regardless of appearance*. Otherwise, they will probably return your photographs to you with a note saying there is nothing on your film but dust specks!

Part Two

A Close-up Look

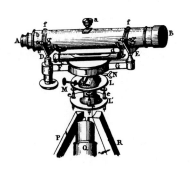

Chapter 8

Selecting Binoculars

© Dennis Mammana

Using binoculars is an excellent next step to studying the heavens. Binoculars will extend your seeing power six to ten times, and they are also extremely lightweight and portable. Better yet, they are relatively inexpensive and can be purchased in any quality department or discount store.

The main purpose of binoculars, of course, is to bring distant subjects nearby for detailed study. In addition to their use for stargazing, they are quite

Above: The constellation of Gemini, the Twins, has several fascinating deep-sky objects visible with binoculars.

valuable for many other activities, such as sightseeing, bird-watching, camping, boating, mountaineering, and photography.

Many varieties and styles of binoculars are available today—each with a different purpose. You can find quality binoculars that don't cost a fortune. Many types look deceptively similar, however, so be sure to evaluate your needs carefully, learn binocular characteristics and functions, and perform some simple tests before making your final choice.

Major Characteristics

All binoculars, no matter what size, type, or price, work on the same principle. They gather light from distant subjects with their objective lenses (in front), and magnify it with their eyepieces (at the rear). Their major characteristics—magnifying power, lens diameter, and field of view—are represented by numbers imprinted on the instrument.

Binoculars are commonly described as 7×50, 7×35, 8×20, and so on. The first number represents the magnifying power of the instrument. The second represents the diameter of the objective lens in millimeters. For example, 7×35 binoculars have 35mm-wide objective lenses and magnify an image seven times.

Another frequently encountered number is the field of view. This is often given as the size of a scene (in feet [meters]) as viewed from a distance of 1,000 yards (900m). Typical fields of view range from about 315 feet (94.5m) to about 640 feet (192m). To convert these to degrees simply divide by 52.5. For example, 640 feet at 1,000 yards equals 12 degrees.

Magnifying power, lens diameter, and field of view are all interrelated. The size of the objective lens is a direct measure of the amount of light it can gather. The more light gathered, the larger the image can be magnified before it deteriorates. The magnifying power, in turn, plays a major role in determining the size of the field of view.

Remember, too, that bigger is not always better when it comes to binoculars. What is important is the relative-light-efficiency (RLE) of the instrument. The greater the RLE, the brighter and clearer the image. (A high RLE is 1; a low RLE is 0.)

To determine the RLE of a particular instrument, simply square the magnifying power (multiply it by itself) and divide the resulting number into the lens diameter. For example, a 7×50 instrument has an RLE of about 1 (or 50 divided by 49). A 10×50 instrument, on the other hand, has an RLE of 0.50 (50 divided by 100) This is much less desirable for stargazing since the light is not used as efficiently as it is by a 7×50.

It is easy to see that the 35mm-diameter lens gathers less light than its 50mm counterpart, but that light is magnified less and produces a brighter image. This point is especially important to consider when selecting binoculars for stargazing.

Types of Binoculars

Two basic types of binoculars are available today: field glasses and prism binoculars. Each type has significant and important differences.

Binoculars gather images of faraway objects and focus them at a point where they can be viewed in detail by the eyes.

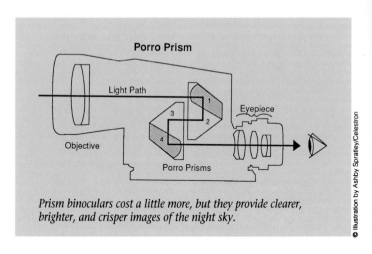

Porro Prism

Light Path

Objective

Eyepiece

Porro Prisms

Prism binoculars cost a little more, but they provide clearer, brighter, and crisper images of the night sky.

Field glasses are also known as opera glasses, theater glasses, or sport glasses. They are simply two low-power refractor telescopes attached together. Light enters the objective lenses, is focused, then is magnified by the eyepiece at the other end.

Prism binoculars are a bit more complex. They also have objective lenses and eyepieces, but inside their sealed barrels lies a complex arrangement of precisely aligned reflective prisms. These prisms bring the light together from the widely spaced objective lenses into our eyes.

Prism binoculars are far better for stargazing than field glasses. Their larger objective-lens diameters provide greater light, higher magnifications, and a generally superior image. Another advantage of prism binoculars over field glasses is that they offer a much wider field of view. These advantages combine to make prism binoculars more expensive than field glasses. Unless your budget restrictions are quite severe, however, prism binoculars are a much better choice.

The differences between field glasses and prism

binoculars are not always immediately obvious to the casual shopper. In fact, field glasses are often shaped and marketed to appear similar to prism binoculars, though the manufacturers are prohibited from using the word "prism" in their promotional material.

There are ways to spot the differences, however. One giveaway is often the spacing of the objective lenses. Field glass objectives are always directly opposite their eyepieces. Prism binoculars' objectives are often set farther apart than their eyepieces.

The only sure way to spot the difference is to look for the prisms themselves. Turn the eyepieces toward a bright light source a few feet away. With your eyes a few inches away from the objectives, look through them; as you do, swing them back and forth slightly. You should see a line of reflections inside, much like a line of automobile headlights coming toward you. If you see no such reflections, the binoculars are not prism binoculars.

Selecting Binoculars

Although this does not hold true for many items found in stores today, price is a good measure of binocular quality. Your final decision, however, should be based not only on price, but on a number of other important factors, including size, weight, field of view, image brightness and quality, focusing range, eye relief, interpupillary distance, lens coating, magnification, and objective diameter.

To help simplify your task, remember that 7×50 binoculars are among the best for astronomical purposes. They provide a large light-gathering power with moderate magnification. Larger 14×70 or 20×80 binoculars are also good choices if you mount them on a tripod. 7×35s are a good general-purpose instrument that are suitable for stargazing, though they are less efficient with their use of light.

When you go shopping for binoculars, always remember to compare similar models and try using them to view similar subjects. Carefully examine the outside casing and glass. Large scratches on the lens surfaces or nicks in the frame are evidence that the instrument has been dropped or mishandled. To inspect the interior condition, aim the eyepieces toward a bright light a few feet away, then look around the inside of each barrel for chipped glass or dirt.

While examining the inside of each barrel, make sure that most or all of the internal glass surfaces are coated. (This is very important, since lens coatings help produce brighter, crisper images with no ghost reflections.) To do so, note the reflection of a nearby fluorescent light off the outer lenses and eyepieces. If the light appears amber or purple, the internal surfaces are coated. Next, observe the internal reflections you saw earlier; if any of them appear brighter or whiter than others, this indicates that the internal surfaces are uncoated.

Next, check the focusing mechanism on the binoculars. Two types of focusing mechanisms are commonly used today: central and independent. A central-focus mechanism has a knob between the barrels that changes the focus of both eyepieces together. This mechanism usually has one eyepiece that can be adjusted for focus differences between the eyes, whereas an independent-focus mechanism requires that each eyepiece be adjusted independently.

Central-focus binoculars are good for general use, particularly if you will be sharing them with other observers, or if the subjects you are observing are less than 100 feet (30m) away. Independent-focus instruments should be used only when you won't be changing the focus very often and/or if you need a particularly rugged and water-resistant instrument. (For stargazing, you'll set the focus for infinity [∞] and should not need to change it to another setting unless someone else uses your binoculars.)

Whichever type of binoculars you select, be certain that the focus mechanism operates smoothly throughout its full range. If it moves firmly at room temperature, it will surely stick in cold weather.

Many binocular eyepieces are adjustable for differences in eye spacing, referred to as the "interpupillary distance." To adjust the interpupillary distance, rotate the barrels on the center post to align the eyepieces comfortably with your eyes. The hinging mechanism should be solid, sturdy, and have a smooth motion throughout its full range. Be certain that when the hinge is adjusted for your eyes it does not pinch your nose.

Next examine the eye relief, that is, the distance your eyes must lie from the eyepieces in order to comfortably see a full field of view. First, look at a distant scene with the binoculars. Now slowly move your eyes back from the eyepieces about an inch (2.5cm). The circular field of view should shrink and become fuzzy on the edges. Slowly move your eyes closer to the eyepieces until the field expands and has a sharp edge again; once

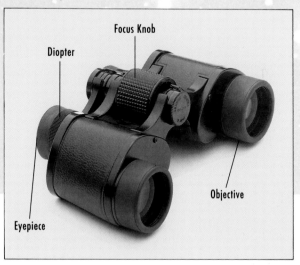

Binoculars are an excellent compromise between the naked eye and a telescope.

© Courtesy of Celestron

Focus Knob

Diopter

Eyepiece

Objective

it does, you have found the correct point for your eyes. To continue moving closer will only result in a narrow field once again. The correct point for your eyes should lie between ¼ and ½ inch (63mm and 1.25cm) from the eyepieces. Sometimes rubber eyecups can be used to define the proper eye placement and help keep out extraneous light.

It is also important to examine the actual image quality that the binoculars produce. To do so, focus them as sharply as possible on some finely detailed object—a sign, tree branches, or a building; a good pair of binoculars will have an extremely sharp focus in the center of its field. Now, swing the binoculars slowly to the side and observe how the image sharpness changes as it approaches the edge of the field. All binoculars tend to show a slight deterioration of sharpness here—especially wide-angle binoculars—but this should only be minimal.

Next, aim the binoculars at some long straight lines—distant telephone wires or boards on the side of a building. Notice if they become distorted or curved near the edge of the field. This effect will be most noticeable in lower-quality or wide-angle binoculars.

Another common problem of binoculars is known as chromatic aberration, that is, the appearance of a colored halo around bright objects. To evaluate this, observe a bright light source such as a streetlight or the moon (**never** the sun). As you move the image toward the edge of the field, notice how prominent this halo becomes. Every pair of binoculars shows this effect to some degree, but the trick is to find one in which it is minimal.

If binoculars have been poorly assembled or mishandled, they may be out of alignment. This can cause eye strain or headaches, no matter how slight the problem. To check the alignment, observe a very distant object through the binoculars, then cover one lens with your hand. Hold the binoculars steady and, with the object at the center of the field, quickly remove your hand. If you momentarily see two images, the two barrels are misaligned. Try the same test again, this time with your eyes a few inches away from the eyepieces.

Finally, let's examine one point that is often overlooked until the binoculars are actually being used: how they feel. Are they heavy or bulky to hold in your hands or to carry around your neck? Do they come with a carrying case? These may not seem like important considerations in the store, but when you are out in the field holding them up to the sky, you may have second thoughts about your choice.

The best way to test binoculars, of course, is to use them to observe the stars themselves. Ask the store manager to borrow a pair overnight; if this is impossible, only purchase binoculars with a money-back guarantee in case they prove unsuitable.

Despite the advertisements you may see, the most expensive, top-of-the-line binoculars may not be the best for you. But, before purchasing one of a lower price range, compare its mechanical and optical properties with a more expensive model. If the differences are ones you can live with, then you can save some money and still meet your needs.

A good alternative to a new pair of binoculars is a good pair of used binoculars, which can be exceptional bargains for those who have time to shop around. It's a good idea to read the classified advertisements of local newspapers, check with amateur astronomy or bird-watching groups, or frequent local flea markets and yard sales.

Still, you should be very careful when shopping for secondhand binoculars. You must closely examine their mechanical and optical components because, in some older "bargain" instruments, even a slight bump may produce two barrels full of loose glass. In addition to the tests outlined in this chapter, try to learn from the owner how the binoculars were used and what kind of care they received.

In the final analysis, astronomical binoculars should be lightweight and portable, provide clear, crisp images, and be reasonably priced. Even a small amount of comparison shopping will greatly improve your chances of finding a durable, quality instrument.

Checklist for Purchasing Astronomical Binoculars

When purchasing astronomical binoculars, keep in mind these guidelines:

- *Choose prism binoculars. They are preferable to field glasses.*
- *The field of view should be as wide as possible.*
- *Choose binoculars with medium magnification (7×).*
- *The lenses should be coated.*
- *The image should be bright and clear.*
- *There should be minimal distortion and chromatic aberration.*
- *The barrels should be parallel.*
- *Your eyes should feel comfortable, and the eyepieces should be the proper distance from your eyes.*
- *The binoculars should be lightweight and easy to hold.*
- *The focusing knob should move smoothly.*

Chapter 9

Selecting a Telescope

© Brian Sullivan

Once you've become familiar with the sky visible to the naked eye and have learned some of its finer points through binoculars, you may feel ready to use a small backyard telescope. Selecting and purchasing one, however, can be confusing and frustrating. Whether you browse department stores, toy and hobby shops, planetarium gift shops, or the catalogs of scientific instrument compa-

Above: Spectacular clusters of stars are just some of the many celestial objects to fall within the range of small backyard telescopes.

nies, you will discover that telescopes come in a bewildering variety of types and sizes, as well as in a range of prices.

Fortunately, there is a way to sort through all the scientific and sales gibberish to select the right telescope, one that will give you and your family great enjoyment and not wind up in a hall closet after only a few outings. Before you rush out and buy a telescope on impulse, stop and ask yourself several questions.

First, are you really ready for a telescope? If you can't yet find your way around the night sky or identify some stars, constellations, or planets, a telescope won't do you much good. Second, what do you wish to look at? Do you want to view the moon and planets, search for faint objects such as star clusters, nebulae, and galaxies, or do you want to watch birds and other terrestrial activity? Finally, and often most important, how much do you want to spend? A good telescope is not a toy. You simply can't get a high-quality instrument for less than $200.

Once you've answered these questions honestly, you've passed the first hurdle. The next step is to understand what a telescope is and how it works. Don't rely on salespeople here. They are often required to sell calculators, coffeepots, and hair dryers as well, and probably don't understand telescopes at all; consequently, they can unknowingly pass on incorrect information that could lead to a poor purchase on your part.

How Telescopes Work

All telescopes work on the same principle. They gather faint light and concentrate it at a point where it is magnified into a finely detailed image.

The most important property of a telescope is not its magnifying power, however, but its ability to gather light. This ability to gather light depends on the size of the telescope's main lens or mirror, known as its "objective." The larger the objective diameter, the more light the telescope can capture. For example, while a 2.4-inch (6cm) (diameter) telescope can see objects 100 times fainter than can the unaided human eye, a 4-inch (10cm) telescope can see objects that are 251 times fainter. Not only does a larger telescope reveal fainter objects, it also presents brighter objects with greater clarity and detail.

Once light is concentrated at the telescope's "focal point," it is then magnified by the eyepiece. The more an image is enlarged, the fainter it becomes. As you might imagine, there exists a maximum practical limit to a telescope's magnifying power. To find the maximum practical limit, just multiply the telescope's diameter in inches by 50 (cm by 20). By this rule of thumb, the maximum usable magnification of a 4-inch (10cm) telescope is about 200×. Beware of a 4-inch telescope that boasts 600 power; any magnification over the theoretical maximum just described is only a sales ploy and is about as useful as the highest numbers on your car's speedometer. The bigger the telescope, the more it can magnify.

Also dependent upon a telescope's size is its ability to resolve fine detail in an image. A 2.4-inch (6cm) telescope can theoretically resolve craters on the moon 4 miles (6.4km) wide, while a 4-inch (10cm) can theoretically resolve craters only 2 miles (3.2km) wide.

Thus, it is fair to say that, when it comes to telescopes, bigger is usually better. But remember, a finely made small telescope will always outperform a poorly made large one.

Types of Telescopes

Though there are many strange-looking varieties of telescopes available today, only two basic types are recommended for the beginner: the refractor and the reflector.

Invented nearly four centuries ago by an unknown Dutch spectacle maker, the refractor is a telescope that resembles a spyglass. Light enters the front of the tube and is bent, or refracted, by the objective lens and is focused at the rear by the eyepiece.

The refractor telescope uses a lens to gather light and create an image at the focal point (a distance f_o away). The eyepiece (with a focal length of f_e) then focuses the light for the eye.

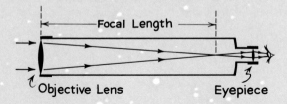

Focal Length

Objective Lens   Eyepiece

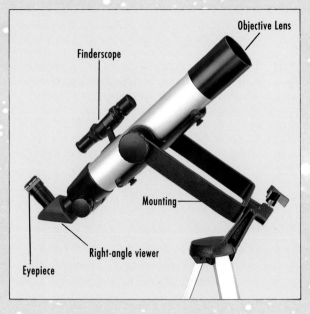

Objective Lens

Finderscope

Mounting

Right-angle viewer

Eyepiece

The refractor has numerous advantages. It is capable of producing high magnifications and often creates razor-sharp images of the moon and planets. It is extremely rugged and resistant to misuse and is quite portable in sizes up to about 4 inches (10cm).

The refractor does have its problems, however. Because its lens cannot focus all colors of light perfectly, its images are often afflicted by chromatic aberration. In addition, refractors are expensive, as high-quality lenses are difficult to make. This makes smaller refractors the norm; the most common diameters are between 2 and 3 inches (5 and 7.5cm). Refractors are an excellent choice for beginners, or for those wishing to concentrate their efforts on the moon, planets, or terrestrial activity.

The other basic type of telescope used today is the reflector, so called because it uses a highly polished mirror to gather starlight. Several styles of reflectors exist, but perhaps the most popular models among beginners are the Newtonian and the rich-field reflectors.

In a Newtonian-style reflector (so named because it was first developed by Isaac Newton in the eighteenth century), light enters its open tube in front. At the back, the light encounters the primary mirror and is reflected back to a smaller, secondary mirror. Here the light is reflected out the side of the tube to the eyepiece.

The other popular style of reflector is the rich-field telescope (RFT). Its relatively low magnifications and exceptionally wide-angle field of view produce brilliant and crisp images of the sky. RFTs do not need a sturdy mounting. In fact, one model—the lightweight Edmund Astroscan—is designed to be cradled in the arms while observing, and it also comes with a strap attachment for easy portability.

Reflectors have many advantages. Since they are relatively inexpensive, a large reflector often can be purchased for the same price or less than a small refractor. Reflectors also give perfect color definition of all images. Not only do they produce stunning views of the moon and planets, their greater light-gathering power makes them excellent for viewing faint star clusters, nebulae, and galaxies as well.

Unfortunately, reflectors have disadvantages, too. They are not as rugged as refractors, and misuse will cause their optics to get out of adjustment. Because their tubes are often open and their optical components exposed, they must always be protected by storing them in their cases.

When comparing refractors and reflectors, it is wise to remember that, in terms of size, the refractor will almost always prove the better instrument. For your money, however, the reflector is the best choice.

Mountings

An important component of a telescope is its mounting. The purpose of the mounting is to hold the telescope steady while it is being used to make observations. A poor mounting will allow wind, a slight bump, or even your walking around to shake the telescope and send the highly magnified image dancing all over the field of view. Few problems destroy star-viewing enthusiasm more quickly than a wobbly mounting.

Many varieties of mountings exist, but there are two basic types: the altitude-azimuth (or alt-az) mounting and the equatorial mounting.

The alt-az mounting is the most common type, and is generally found on instruments of 3 inches (7.5cm) in diameter or smaller. This mounting is similar to a camera tripod and can allow the telescope to be moved in two directions: in altitude (vertically) and in azimuth (horizontally).

The alt-az mounting is usually quite sufficient for observations of terrestrial objects, or for beginning glances at the moon, planets, and other bright objects. It is not made for serious observing, however, for two separate motions must be continually adjusted to compensate for the rotation of the Earth when following objects across the sky.

The equatorial mounting, on the other hand, is

A reflector gathers light with a mirror, and uses a secondary mirror to reflect the light out the side of the tube where it can be viewed with the eye.

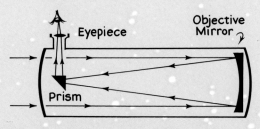

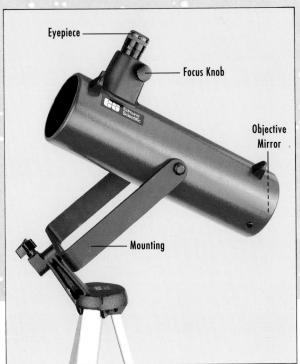

Different mountings are available for telescopes and provide different capabilities. For astronomical observations, however, an equatorial mounting is best.

designed to simulate the motion of the Earth exactly. With only one sweeping motion (manually, or with an automatic motor drive) the observer can easily track an object during the night. In addition, the equatorial mounting often comes equipped with setting circles inscribed with celestial coordinates to help aim the telescope toward extremely faint objects.

The equatorial mounting is designed for more serious stargazing, and is considerably more expensive than the alt-az mounting. It also takes a bit of practice to master the equatorial's operation, but the freedom and flexibility this mounting offers are worth the effort. An equatorial is also a must for anyone hoping eventually to take long-exposure telescopic photographs of the heavens.

Finderscopes, Eyepieces, and Sun Filters

When purchasing a telescope for the first time, you will undoubtedly encounter numerous accessories that can "enhance" your observing pleasure. For many people, that first telescope will be challenge enough—you won't need more gadgets to complicate matters. The only two accessories you will need at first are a finderscope and a set of eyepieces. Fortunately, most beginning telescopes come equipped with these as standard equipment.

Telescopes with magnifying powers of more than 20× should be equipped with a finderscope, that is, a small 5× or 6× telescope mounted parallel to the main tube near the eyepiece holder. Its exceptionally wide field of view and central cross hairs are necessary for locating and centering objects for study in the main instrument.

Eyepieces are as important as finderscopes since no image can be seen without them. The particular eyepiece being used also determines the magnifying power of a telescope. If you look at the eyepiece, you'll notice a number printed there; this is not the eyepiece's magnification but its focal length. To determine its magnification, simply divide that number into the focal length of the telescope (usually printed on the tube or in the instruction manual). For example, a 900mm focal-length telescope with a 20mm focal-length eyepiece would produce a magnification of 900 divided by 20, or 45×.

Many telescopes come with three eyepieces, one of low-power magnification (20×–50×); one of medium power (50×–100×); and one of high power (100× or more). Low-power eyepieces are used much more frequently than high power ones. They produce a wider field of view and are more useful in locating and observing faint objects. High-power eyepieces have a narrow field of view and are useful only when the object you are viewing is bright and the night is steady.

Some telescopes come equipped with a Barlow

lens—a long tube that doubles the magnification of any eyepiece used with it. Barlow lenses are nice to have, but they are seldom useful on high-power eyepieces.

Another item commonly sold with a small telescope is a sun filter. This filter screws onto the bottom of the eyepiece, the same place where the sun's light is concentrated. **These filters are extremely dangerous: they can melt, burn, or crack and throw a scorching beam of sunlight directly into your eye, which will cause instant blindness.** If you purchase a telescope with one of these sun filters, destroy and discard it at once. Safe methods of observing the sun are outlined in chapter 12.

Moon filters, on the other hand, are perfectly safe when observing the moon. While these filters are not necessary, you may find that they cut down glare,

Checklist for Purchasing an Astronomical Telescope

When purchasing an astronomical telescope, keep in mind these guidelines:

- *Make sure the image is bright and clear.*
- *There should be minimal distortion and chromatic aberration.*
- *The tripod and the mounting should be sturdy.*
- *The controls should be easy to reach.*
- *The controls and focusing knob should move smoothly.*
- *The telescope should be lightweight and portable.*
- *The finderscope should be attached to the telescope.*
- *The telescope should come with accessory eyepieces.*

improve the contrast of a bright moon, and make your viewing more comfortable.

While fine telescopes may be bought off the showroom floor or directly out of a catalog, there is no substitute for testing one outdoors. If you can get permission from the store manager to take a telescope home for an evening, do so. The experience will pay off immensely.

Testing a Telescope

While it's still light outdoors, set up the telescope according to the instruction manual, then aim it toward some distant mountains or radio tower and lock it down. Insert a low-power eyepiece and focus until the image becomes sharp. The enlarged image may be inverted, but don't be alarmed. This is a normal property of most telescopes and makes little difference when viewing the sky.

Now insert a medium-power eyepiece and refocus, holding the telescope as steady as possible. When the telescope is released, you should see the image vibrating in the eyepiece. A vibration time of 6 to 8 seconds after release is normal. Anything longer than 10 to 12 seconds indicates that the mounting is poor.

Later that evening, with all outdoor lighting off, aim the telescope toward the moon and focus it. (If the moon is not visible, aim toward a bright star instead.) The image should appear bright and free of distortion, with no ghost images anywhere in the field. If haziness, milkiness, or excessive rainbow colors are present, the telescope or eyepiece may be poorly made (assuming, of course, that the sky itself is not hazy). Remember to try all eyepieces to check their quality.

If taking the telescope home from the store is impossible, at least try to use it outside the store. Be careful not to look through a glass window at anything, since that will only distort the image and leave you with an inaccurate impression of the telescope's capabilities. Also be sure to inspect the mechanical parts of the instrument. Is the mounting well built and sturdy? Are the tripod legs thick and heavy? Is the mounting smooth in its motion, and are its controls easy to find and operate? If the mechanical parts and tripod are well built and durable, it is a safe bet that the optics are, too. If you can get the opinion of a more experienced amateur, do so; it never hurts to get direct advice before making a major purchase.

If the prices or sizes of telescopes available are beyond your reach, don't despair. There are good alternatives. You may be able to find a high-quality second-hand telescope at a reasonable price. Advertisements for secondhand telescopes appear occasionally in local newspapers or in the newsletters of local amateur astronomy groups.

You can also make your own telescope. This is an inexpensive way to obtain a large telescope, but the process is time consuming and is not for those who lack patience. Nor is making your own telescope recommended for those who have never observed through or operated one before. Check with your local library, planetarium, or amateur astronomy group for telescope-making classes in your area.

Finally, perhaps the most common error of first-time telescope users is an unrealistic expectation of what a telescope can show. Swirling galaxies, undulating clouds of gas and dust, and brilliantly colored planets promoted in photographs are just that—photographs—taken through the world's largest telescopes. The view through a small backyard telescope is understandably much more modest. But the incredible feeling of actually peering many thousands or millions of light-years into space simply cannot be inspired by a photograph.

If you are careful to evaluate your interests, learn how a telescope works, and select an appropriate model, your telescope will reveal remarkable sights and provide a lifetime of enjoyment for you and your family.

Chapter 10

Gearing Up for Stargazing

© Greg Vaughn/Tom Stack & Associates

To avoid wasting precious observing time, you should carefully plan out your night's session before going outdoors. Make a list of the objects and phenomena you hope to see, and outline any special features you wish to study. To do this you'll need to consider such factors as time of night and season of year, the weather prospects, the light pollution in your area, the phase of the moon and

Above: An amateur astronomer begins at twilight to set up for the night's study of the heavens.

where it appears, and even the local terrain of your observing site.

In other words, ask yourself whether the objects you'd like to see are visible at your site at this time of night during this particular season. Are they high enough in the sky to see over trees, houses, and mountains? Are they bright enough to see, or will the moon or light pollution interfere? What if the weather turns bad? Do you have a contingency plan to take advantage of the new conditions?

After considering these factors, plan your night's observing sequence from west to east. This way, as the Earth turns on its axis it will carry objects over you and you can observe objects high overhead all night long.

Next, decide on the equipment you will need to accomplish your goals for the night. Will binoculars be suitable or will you need a telescope? Will you need low- or high-power eyepieces? If you're traveling away from home to observe, you may wish to concentrate on observations that can be done with minimal equipment. You will also need to determine whether you should take supplies such as star maps, a red flashlight, spare batteries, observing log and pencil, warm clothing, a thermos of a hot beverage, or a portable chair and/or table.

Setting Up

Arrive at your observing site well before dark to allow plenty of time to learn the terrain and get set up. Locate a solid piece of ground and assemble your telescope. Try to avoid working on asphalt, since the heat it has accumulated from the sun during the day radiates away at night and may cause distortions in front of your telescope. Make sure your telescope is level and that the tripod is solidly assembled.

Your next task should be to align the finderscope with your main instrument. To do this, find a very distant object, such as a mountaintop or radio antenna, and aim your telescope in its direction. Start with a low-power eyepiece. Once you have found the object in the telescope, switch to a higher-power eyepiece and align it so that a recognizable feature is directly in the center of its field of view. Lock down the telescope firmly so it can't move.

Now loosen the finderscope and point it so that its cross hairs are aimed at the same object. Lock the finderscope down and look through the telescope eyepiece to make sure the instrument hasn't moved. You may have to do some fine tuning to make sure that the two eyepieces are aimed at the same object.

When you are done, your finderscope will be aligned so that it can help you locate objects in the sky efficiently. Put a low-power eyepiece in the telescope, and you should easily see a magnified image of the object. Remember: never try to locate an object with a high-power eyepiece in the telescope, and always focus and align your finderscope in daylight with a distant, static object. If you try to focus it with a star or the moon, its motion across the sky will only make the job more difficult.

As the sky darkens, you can enjoy the sunset, watch the Earth's shadow rise in the east, or locate some of the brighter stars and planets. Meanwhile, your telescope's optics are adjusting to the cooling air. This cooling is necessary for two reasons: it reduces the heat escaping from the telescope, heat that can cause distorted images, and it reduces the chances that dew will form on the optics.

As darkness falls, your eyes will gradually become dark adapted. Use the time to focus your telescope properly. To do this, find a star of 2nd or 3rd magnitude and aim your telescope in its direction. Keep in mind that no telescope in existence can magnify the image of a star—stars are just too far away. Turn the telescope focus knob one way and watch as the star turns larger and fuzzier. Now turn it the other way and watch again. If the star looks like a fuzzy ring, the telescope is not focused properly. When the telescope is properly adjusted, the star should appear as a tiny and sharp point of light.

Once you've focused the telescope, use it to check the seeing and transparency of the sky. Aim it toward a star high overhead and notice how it twinkles. Then aim it toward a star of similar brightness low in the sky. You should see a significant difference in the stars' scintillation. If the seeing or transparency of the sky is not as good as you feel is necessary to complete your observing program, you may need to adjust your plans.

Tricks of the Trade

As you observe the night sky, you'll want to coax the best from your telescope and your eyes. The following astronomical tricks of the trade should help you out.

First, remain dark adapted. Resist the temptation to use any light other than red to read notes or star maps. Avoid looking into car headlights, streetlights, or any other white light at all costs.

Second, to get the best view through the telescope, make sure your eye is positioned correctly behind the eyepiece. You should see a clear and undistorted circular field of view with the object you wish to observe inside. If your observing site is far from light pollution and if there is no moon in the sky, the sky will appear nearly black, so this field of view may be difficult to see. If, on the other hand, there is scattered light in the sky, the field will appear gray and will reduce your ability to see really faint objects.

Third, use averted vision when observing faint objects. This method of observation works as well with a telescope as it does with the naked eye. Locate the object you wish to view in the center of your field and glance off to its side. In this way you'll be able to study the object's structure, or see detail that would be lost if you tried looking directly at it.

Finally, keep both eyes open when observing through a telescope. This is difficult at first and requires quite a bit of practice, but closing one eye and squinting is hard on the facial muscles and will make you tire more quickly. So keep both eyes open and concentrate only on the eye looking into the eyepiece (this is much easier when it is extremely dark and there is no scattered light on the ground).

Chapter 11

Observing the Moon

© Lick Observatory

Perhaps the first object most people ever see through a small backyard telescope is the moon. It has been said that the moon is "looked over, then overlooked," for once people see it, they tend to lose interest. This doesn't have to be true. The moon is one of the most exciting celestial objects to view again and again.

Above: These two photographs illustrate how the east-west libration of the moon enables the viewers to see more of its surface.

You will find that even the best of photographs taken with the world's largest telescopes cannot compare to the view of the moon you can get directly through your backyard telescope. The reason for this is that all photographs capture not only the moon itself, but the turbulent air between the moon and the camera. Any photograph will "remember" the distortion caused by wavering air during the exposure and, therefore, is bound to be slightly blurry. But a view of the moon with the human eye remains sharp, even though the eye experiences the same amount of atmospheric turbulence; the eye sees a series of instantaneous images, and each separate view "forgets" the turbulence seen in the previous moment.

Lunar Features

Learning the lunar features is not difficult. In fact, it's quite fun to take a tour across the mountains and craters of the moon with your telescope and a good lunar map by your side.

Take a look through your eyepiece, and you'll see the colorfully named dark lunar maria, such as the Lake of the Dead, the Ocean of Storms, and others, which are actually dried lava plains left over from the early days of our moon's life. The maria may be the result of the constant bombardment of large rocks from space that once devastated the moon. As the rocks hit the moon, some of them broke open the moon's crust, allowing lava to flow toward the surface.

Nearly a third of the moon's face is covered with these remnant lava flows. But they are not entirely flat as they first may appear to be. Look more closely and you will see ripples in their surfaces; the ripples are waves in the original lava that were frozen in place when it finally solidified.

Around the edges of the maria, as well as elsewhere, you might see long mountain ranges. The lunar mountains are often named after ranges on Earth—the Alps, the Appenines, and so on—although some are larger

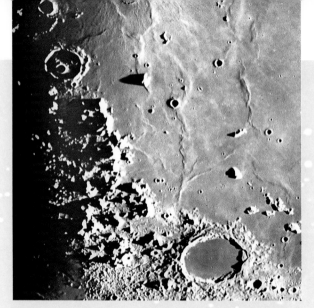

The moon's terminator, which divides the dark and light sides, highlights the geographical aspects of the surface. This mountain range is called "the Alps."

than their Earthly counterparts. Galileo calculated that some of these mountains were as high as 4 miles (6.4km).

Around the lunar surface, you may also spot deep cracks, rilles, and valleys. Some have colorful names, such as Hyginus Cleft, Alpine Valley, and the Straight Wall. In fact, you will see countless craters everywhere; craters abound on the moon's surface. Most are impact features, caused by falling debris left over from the formation of our solar system 5 billion years ago. Most are visible through a small telescope and range from only a few miles to up to 150 miles (240km) across.

As you study the variety and number of craters on the moon, you will notice that many of them are actually craters within other craters. Those craters on the inside are the youngest craters; for anything present there would have been destroyed upon formation of the larger, outer crater eons earlier. You'll also notice that some craters are partially covered, and once in a while you will spot a "ghost" crater. Ghost craters show only the upper crater walls, because their deep insides are completely covered with the solidified lava.

Many lunar craters also have a mountain peak at their centers. It may not seem possible that a rock could hit the moon and form the crater without destroying the mountain peak, but what occurred was that the moun-

Copernicus, one of the largest lunar craters, stretches about fifty-six miles across and its walls tower more that three miles above the lunar surface.

Courtesy of Meade Instruments

tain was actually formed with the crater. This happened in much the same way as the splash that occurs when you drop a pebble into a glass of water, except that these lunar splashes solidified from molten rock to form central peaks in many of the moon's craters.

Some of the largest lunar craters—such as Tycho and Copernicus—actually have bright streaks emanating radially outward from them. These rays, it is believed, were formed by ejected material that was blasted outward from the tremendous impact that formed the craters. These rays are particularly striking during a gibbous or full moon.

Viewing the Moon

One common misconception of beginning stargazers is that the best time to view the moon is during its full phase. Nothing could be further from the truth. The full moon is illuminated head on by the sun, and at that time shadows of lunar features are virtually nonexistent. (The shadows provide contrast between most lunar features and the surrounding landscape. Without the shadows, the moon appears flat and dull.)

When you view the moon depends entirely on what you are trying to see. If you wish to see the darkened moon in the light of earthshine, you must view the thin crescent moon shortly after sunset or before sunrise. If you wish to view the dark lunar maria, you may wish to view during a gibbous or full moon, when the moon's surface is fully illuminated by the sun.

The very best time to view the moon, however, is during its thick-crescent or quarter phases. This is when sunlight falls on the lunar surface at a steep angle and creates long shadows of the lunar craters, mountains, valleys, and rilles. Shadows appear along the "terminator," the line separating the light and dark sides of the moon.

In other words, the terminator marks the boundary between lunar day and lunar night, as well as representing the terrain that shows the longest and darkest shadows. If you study the shadows along the terminator, you will discover very quickly that they change daily. The reason for this is that, as the moon orbits the Earth, the sun shines on the moon's surface from slightly different angles. These shadows seem to change from night to night, making new features continually visible to us on Earth.

But if you look closely, you will discover that these features can sometimes change within hours, and sometimes even faster. The place to look for these changes is not on the bright side of the terminator, but on the dark side. Occasionally, you might see a bright spot peeking out of the lunar darkness as a mountaintop catches the rising sun's light. If you watch it for a while with high power, you may actually see it change within minutes as sunlight streams down the mountain's slopes.

The Wobbling Moon

As you observe the moon month after month, you will notice that the same face continually faces the Earth, for the moon rotates on its axis at the same rate at which it revolves about our planet. It would seem that the side of the moon facing away from us is never seen from here.

But this statement is not exactly true. In fact, anyone can see more than half of the moon's surface over the course of time—if they know how to look. It is possible to see more of the moon because its orbit around the Earth is not a perfect circle, but an ellipse, and its speed, therefore, is not constant. When the moon is closest to the Earth (referred to as "perigee") it moves more quickly than when it is farthest from the Earth ("apogee"). As a result, it is possible to get a peek around the eastern and western limbs of the moon at about two-week intervals. We can also glimpse around its northern and southern edges, for the moon's orbit around the Earth is tipped at about 5 degrees. This combination of motions actually allows us to see up to 59 percent of the moon's surface over time. The moon's far side, however, remains forever hidden from our view.

Chapter 12

Observing the Sun

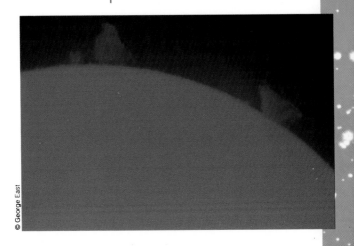

© George East

The sun is the nearest star to us. A body made mostly of hydrogen gases, the sun has a surface temperature of some 10,000°F (about 6,000°C). There is no solid place to stand on the sun, for its surface, or photosphere, is merely the visible edge of its luminous disk.

The sun is but an average-sized star, with a diameter of some 865,000 miles (1,384,000km). It burns not by fire, but by nuclear fusion. Deep in its core,

Above: Huge gaseous eruptions on the sun, called prominences, are visible with specialized (and expensive) hydrogen-alpha filters.

where temperatures soar to more than 10 million°F (6 million°C), hydrogen atoms speed around, slamming so hard into one another that they fuse and form helium. In the process, energy is released in the form of light and heat. Eventually, that energy works its way out of the sun and radiates into space. Some of this energy makes its way to the Earth, where it warms our world, drives our weather, and makes life possible on our planet.

In addition, the sun is constantly throwing particles of hydrogen gas into space. Each second the sun loses 4.5 million tons (4 million t) of material. In the 8.3 minutes it takes light to speed from the sun to the Earth, the sun loses more than 2 billion tons (1.8 billion t) of material. Yet, even at this tremendous rate, the sun has been burning for 5 billion years, and is expected to continue for 5 billion more.

Because the sun is the only star we can see up close, it is exciting to observe with small telescopes. Something is always happening on the sun, but care must be taken to observe it safely.

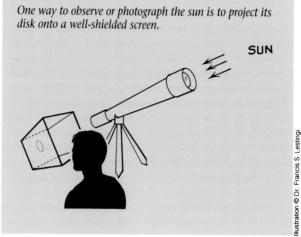

One way to observe or photograph the sun is to project its disk onto a well-shielded screen.

SUN

Safety First

The sun is extremely dangerous to observe. Never look directly at the sun with the naked eye, binoculars, or a telescope. Its intense visible light and its invisible ultraviolet and infrared radiations need only an instant to burn the retina and cause blindness. Even during a partial solar eclipse, when part of the sun is blocked by the moon, enough radiation is emitted that blindness can result instantly.

Sun filters that attach to your telescope's eyepiece are extremely dangerous and must never be used. If your telescope comes with an eyepiece sun filter, destroy and discard it at once. There are safe ways, both indirect and direct, to view the sun.

Indirect Observations

Eyepiece projection is one technique for observing the sun indirectly. Set up your telescope outdoors and let its temperature come to equilibrium with the outside air—this should take about a half hour or so. Now, aim the instrument toward the sun, but not by looking through the finderscope. (In fact, you might wish to remove the finderscope entirely, or cover its objective end with a cap to prevent a potential disaster.) Watch the shadow of the telescope tube on the ground until it changes from an elongated oval to a circle; when it becomes a circle, that means the sunlight is streaming directly down the tube.

Now hold a piece of white cardboard behind the eyepiece; you should see the sun's disk projected onto it. If you don't, you may need to adjust the telescope's position slightly. But, remember, do not look through the telescope. When the sun's image comes into view on the cardboard, turn the focusing knobs until the projected image is sharp. Turn the telescope away or cover it every few minutes to avoid heat buildup inside its tube.

You may eventually wish to enclose your white projection screen in a partially closed cardboard box painted flat black on the inside. This will reduce the scattered

Many techniques for observing the sun are available, but none is safer than indirect viewing.

© Dennis Milon

light on the screen, and increase the sharpness and contrast of the solar image while still allowing you and others to view the sun safely.

Direct Observations

There are solar filters on the market that allow direct observation of the sun, but they are expensive and must be used with care.

No filter will work if it is placed at the eyepiece of a telescope. Doing so only invites trouble, since it is here that the light and heat of the sun is concentrated before entering the eye. The tremendous heat buildup may burn, crack, or explode these filters.

The only safe filters are those that are placed between the instrument and the sun. In other words, by placing a filter over the *objective* end of a telescope or binoculars, the light and heat is kept out of the instrument in the first place, avoiding a potential disaster.

Sunglasses, mylar from balloons, smoked glass, neutral density filters, crossed polarized filters, and other homemade devices may appear to cut the sun's glare, but still may cause blindness: the reason for this is that it is not visible light that causes eye damage, but invisible ultraviolet and infrared radiation. Any solar filter you use must virtually eliminate these light sources, and no homemade filter can do this.

Safe solar filters can be obtained as specially coated mylar or glass. These are placed over the objective end of the telescope or binoculars and allow only one-millionth of the sun's radiation to pass through. Both types are good filters; each has its advantages and disadvantages.

Specially coated mylar is very thin, lightweight, and produces extremely sharp, crisp images of the sun. But it can be damaged quite easily and also produces a slightly bluish image of the sun. Glass filters, on the other hand, are stronger and provide a more natural yellowish or orange image. But the images glass filters produce may not be quite as sharp as those produced by mylar. Glass filters also cost about twice as much as mylar filters.

Filters that screw onto an eyepiece should never be used to view the sun. Only those that cover the telescope's front end are safe.

Courtesy of Celestron

What to Look For

There is a great deal of interesting phenomena to observe on the sun. The sun is a constantly changing place, and is ideal for amateur astronomers to study—especially those whose night sky is washed out by light pollution.

The best time to observe the sun is often during the few hours after sunrise, before ground heat begins to build up. Avoid observing the sun over a hot roof or street; in fact, the best possible observing site is a wide field of grass.

You will discover quickly that the sun's disk is not featureless, but blemished with sunspots, dark markings that appear scattered around its face. A close look at a sunspot with high magnification shows that it has a dark inner section (umbra) and a light outer part (penumbra). No one knows exactly what sunspots are, but they are believed to be cooler areas of the sun's atmosphere that occur in the regions of magnetic storms. Most sunspots are many times larger than our entire Earth.

Sunspots are not static. They change over days or weeks. Sometimes they grow in size, and sometimes they break up and disappear completely. You can follow their progress by sketching or photographing the sun on your cardboard projection screen.

Over time, you will notice that sunspots seem to march across the sun's disk together, as new ones appear over the opposite solar limb. This occurs because the sun itself is rotating. As the sun is a non-solid body, it does not spin at the same speed everywhere on its disk. Its equatorial regions rotate once every 25 days or so, while those near its north or south poles may take up to 40 days to go around.

In addition, the sunspots you see at the solar edge may appear to be more elongated than those at its center. That's because you are viewing them from a different perspective. Those at the center are viewed directly from above. But those on the edge are being carried by the sun's rotation from or toward the back side of the solar disk; you see these sunspots as they are turning toward or away from you, so they appear to be distorted.

The number of sunspots change from day to day, from week to week, and even from year to year. In fact, their numbers increase and decrease over an approximate 11-year cycle, known as the "sunspot cycle." The cycle is approximate, and variations of several years can occur.

Sunspots are not the only features visible on the sun's face. Look carefully at the limb of the sun. You may notice that the limb appears slightly darker—even slightly redder—than the middle of the sun's disk. This is known as "limb-darkening," and it occurs because the sun is a sphere of gas whose energy-producing region is near its center. When you look toward the sun's limb, you are viewing its upper atmosphere where no energy is being produced. Because it produces no energy, it is natural that the upper atmosphere appears darker than the center of the sun's disk.

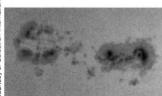

Sunspots provide exciting and constantly changing features on the otherwise bland disk of the sun.

Bright irregular patches near the sun's limb are called "faculae." Faculae are hot gases rising to the top of the sun's atmosphere, and are best visible at the solar limb, for the contrast is greater than at the center of the solar disk.

Another feature of the sun is known as granulation. Huge convection cells, or bubbles, transport heat from below the sun's visible disk out into space; these appear as bright specks on the sun. Conversely, the sun returns cooler gases downward, and these appear as darker specks. Combined, these convection cells give the sun a lemon-peel appearance that is visible on a good clear day. But since most of these granules are only about 600 miles (about 1,000km) across (compared to the sun's 865,000-mile [1,384,000km] diameter), they are extremely small, low-contrast phenomena, and can be seen only during excellent seeing conditions.

The sun is indeed a dynamic and ever-changing orb that you can watch and study with very little equipment. Just remember the extreme importance of viewing this star safely.

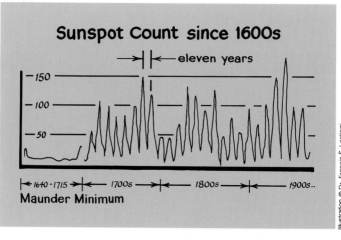

Illustration © Dr. Francis S. Lestingi

Chapter 13

Observing the Planets

© NASA/FPG International

Observing the planets is most enjoyable, but to see any detail at all, you need a telescope, good seeing, and lots of patience.

A telescope reveals that a planet does not appear as a point of light as does a star. Instead, a planet appears as a disk, and if you watch it for days or weeks, you will notice that it moves among the stars. Planets normally move toward the east, but will move toward the west during times of opposition.

When observing planets, atmospheric turbulence

Above: The Voyager spacecraft revealed Saturn and its moons as a spectacular system of alien worlds.

tends to blur fine detail. While this turbulence makes stars appear to twinkle, it does not affect planets as much, for planets do not appear as point sources of light, but as disks. Planets instead seem to waver slightly beneath the effect of the atmosphere.

The secret to seeing fine detail on planets is to use high magnifications and carefully watch a planet's disk as the air moves about in front of it. Occasionally, the turbulence will steady for an instant or so, which will provide you with a spectacularly clear, sharp image.

The Inner Planets: Mercury and Venus

The inner planets, Mercury and Venus, can be seen only at dawn and dusk, for they lie closer to the sun than the Earth, and always appear in its direction.

Mercury is the most elusive of all planets. Rarely visible in complete darkness, this body is so small and so distant (at best some 90 million miles [144 million km] away from the Earth) that it appears to small backyard telescopes as only a tiny disk. Rarely, if ever, is any detail visible. Of all the planets, Mercury suffers the most from atmospheric turbulence. Because it lies so close to the sun, Mercury can be seen only near the horizon—where atmospheric turbulence is the greatest. This, coupled with the fact that it appears to us as such a small disk, makes our view of Mercury tremendously distorted.

On the other hand, Venus—the other inner planet— is much more interesting to watch. Venus can appear higher in the sky than Mercury; sometimes it even appears in total darkness hours after sunset or before sunrise. It's best to observe Venus when it is high in the sky.

Opposite page: Through a small telescope, Mercury and Venus often appear as little more than tiny white dots. Look carefully, however, and you might see them displaying a crescent phase like the moon. Inset: Photographs of Mercury and Venus taken through a fairly powerful backyard telescope.

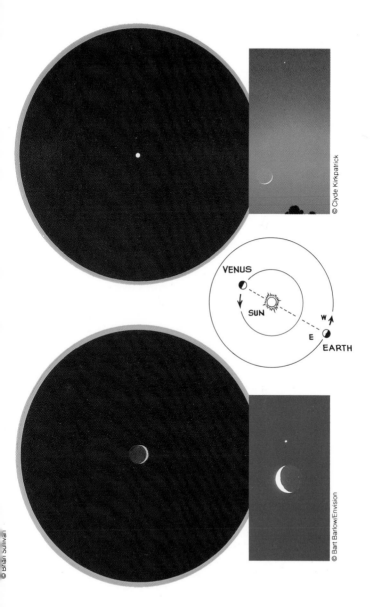

VENUS

SUN

W

E

EARTH

© Clyde Kirkpatrick

© Bart Barlow/Envision

© Brian Sullivan

Venus is the Earth's twin in terms of size and mass, but that's where the similarity ends. If you look at Venus with a small telescope, you will see no detail at all, as this planet is covered by clouds of carbon dioxide and carbon monoxide. Beneath these clouds is a world where temperatures hover near 900°F (500°C), atmospheric pressures exceed the weight of water a mile (1.6km) beneath terrestrial oceans, and rains of sulfuric acid condense out of the Venusian clouds.

Venus can often be seen sparkling brilliantly in the dawn or dusk sky because its white clouds reflect nearly all sunlight that falls on them. Occasionally, as Venus orbits the sun, you can see it show phases much like the moon. When Venus lies on the opposite side of the sun, it is at its most distant point from the Earth. This position is called "superior conjunction," and it is at this point that it appears as a full disk.

But as Venus swings round the sun, sunlight falls on it from different angles. It then grows in size and also changes its phase. As it approaches its position between the Earth and the sun—known as "inferior conjunction"—Venus appears as a large, thin crescent when looked at through a telescope or even binoculars. Sometimes, if you locate Venus before it gets completely dark, you might even be able to spot its crescent with the naked eye.

The Outer Planets

All of the known remaining planets in our solar system are farther from the sun than the Earth. As a result, they can be seen at any time of the night, and often appear very high in the sky. These planets are much farther away than the inner planets. Most of them are larger planets, and produce spectacular images, even in small, backyard telescopes. In addition, because the outer planets are farther from the sun than the Earth, we see only their gibbous and full phases.

The best time to observe the outer planets is when they are in near opposition to the Earth. It is at this time that the Earth and a planet are closest together, and that the planet appears on the opposite side of the sky from the sun. This means that the planet will rise at sunset and set at sunrise, as well as appear much larger in your telescope's field of view.

Mars: The Red Planet

Mars is a very small planet, barely half the size of Earth, and often shows very little detail to a small telescope. At or near opposition, however, Mars can show its orange surface and one or two white ice caps at its poles. You may also notice some dark markings across its face.

Since Mars rotates on its axis once every 24 hours, you can watch it turn slowly during the course of the

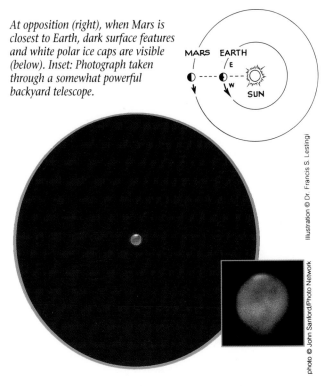

At opposition (right), when Mars is closest to Earth, dark surface features and white polar ice caps are visible (below). Inset: Photograph taken through a somewhat powerful backyard telescope.

bottom illustration © Brian Sullivan

Illustration © Dr. Francis S. Lestingi

photo © John Sanford/Photo Network

Even through a small telescope, an observer can see Jupiter's pastel cloud bands and its four brightest moons. Inset: Photograph of Jupiter taken through a powerful backyard telescope.

night. If you don't see any surface features, it may be because the planet is too distant, your telescope is not powerful enough, or the planet is engulfed in a planet-wide dust storm. These dust storms kick up occasionally and blow reddish soil around the planet, masking all of its features. Sometimes a blue or orange filter at the eyepiece will help show features on Mars.

Jupiter: The Giant Planet

Eleven times larger than Earth, Jupiter is the most spectacular planet to view with a small telescope. You can see its colorful cloud bands streaking from east to west across its disk. If you look carefully, you will notice that Jupiter is not perfectly round, but slightly flattened. This phenomena is caused by Jupiter's rapid rotation—it makes a full rotation in about 10 hours—which causes its gaseous atmosphere to flatten.

One of Jupiter's features that is often visible is the Great Red Spot. Known as a gigantic hurricane some three times larger than Earth, the Red Spot can often be seen as a rosy-colored marking among the clouds of Jupiter. Because Jupiter rotates so rapidly, it is easy to see this or any other feature move across its face during the night.

In fact, because of Jupiter's rapid rate of rotation, its face will appear to change completely in only 5 hours. On a long night, if Jupiter is at opposition, you could begin your observations at sunset and continue until dawn while watching the entire planet rotate in front of you.

Perhaps even more interesting to watch are Jupiter's four large moons. These moons appear as bright stars that lie in a nearly straight line across the planet's equatorial region. Galileo discovered them in 1610 and, in his honor, they are now known as the Galilean moons. The innermost moon is known as Io, and it shines with a slightly orange color. Next outward is Europa, then Ganymede, followed by Callisto.

If you sketch the positions of the moons relative to the planet, you will discover that they move from night to night as they orbit Jupiter. Sometimes, depending on their relative positions, they can actually be seen to move in only minutes. As they move behind Jupiter, they may pass into the planet's giant shadow and disappear for a while—thus experiencing an eclipse. They also may pass in front of the planet and cast their own shadows onto the cloud tops. These phenomena can be seen quite often with high magnification; when they occur, watch for the shadows and moons to move across the planet's face during the evening.

Saturn: The Ringed Planet

Far beyond Jupiter, about 1 billion miles (1.6 billion km) away, lies Saturn. Saturn's most significant feature, of course, is its spectacular rings.

The rings of Saturn are about two and a half times larger than the planet's body. They are quite easy to see, even through a low-powered telescope. On a good clear night with good seeing, you may discover two or three

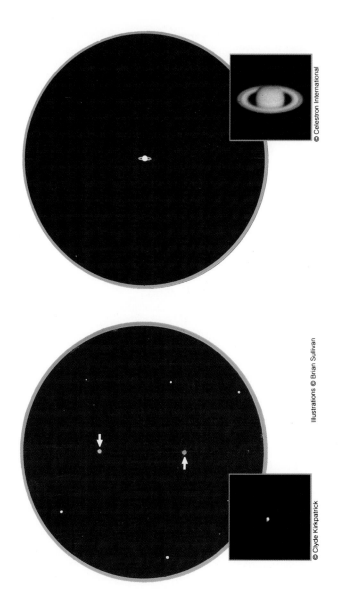

© Celestron International

Illustrations © Brian Sullivan

© Clyde Kirkpatrick

rings divided by dark regions. The rings appear quite solid—almost as if you could drive a car around them. In reality, there are many thousands of individual rings, each made up of billions of chunks of ice and rock whirling around the planet at tens of thousands of miles per hour. Because the rings are not solid, you can occasionally see stars shining through them as Saturn passes by.

While these spectacular rings are nearly 200,000 miles (320,000 km) across, they are only a few miles thick and are tipped about 27 degrees to our line of sight. Because Saturn orbits the sun, our view of the rings changes every 15 years or so. Sometimes, as in 1988, we get the best possible view of the rings. Other times, the view is poor, as in 1981, when the rings were turned almost edge on to our line of sight; to even the largest telescopes in the world, these thin rings seemed to disappear. The rings are now closing down to our view, and will disappear around 1996, but will reach their maximum tilt again in 2003.

Uranus, Neptune, and Pluto: The Remaining Planets

Uranus and Neptune lie far beyond the Earth; they are 2 to 3 billion miles (3.2 to 4.8 billion km) away. These planets are extremely faint in our sky, and are very difficult for beginners to find.

Uranus lies just below the threshold of naked-eye visibility, although sometimes around its opposition, it can become visible. Both Uranus and Neptune appear as barely perceptible disks to even large telescopes. No detail at all is ever visible on these worlds.

All detail we've ever seen on these worlds has come courtesy of the *Voyager 2* spacecraft, which flew past

Opposite, top: Saturn shows its spectacular ring system. Inset: Photograph of Saturn taken through a fairly powerful backyard telescope. Opposite, bottom: Through a small telescope, Uranus appears as a faint blue-green speck among the stars. Neptune appears the same, but much fainter. Inset: Photo of Uranus taken through a telescope.

Uranus in 1986 and past Neptune in 1989. Uranus was revealed as a 16,000-mile- (26,200km) wide globe of hydrogen and helium with virtually no atmospheric features at all. Neptune, nearly the same size as Uranus, was shown to be similar in composition but with visible clouds and storm systems in its atmosphere.

Pluto, a tiny planet, lies some 3 billion miles (4.8 billion km) away. Pluto has never been visited by spacecraft from Earth, so we don't know what its surface is like, though its temperature is likely to hover near −369°F (−223°C). It can be seen easily only with telescopes 16 inches (40cm) across or larger. Even then, Pluto appears as only a faint point of light.

The Planets of Our Solar System

Mercury

*Average distance from the sun: 35 million miles
    (57.9 million km)
Equatorial diameter: 2,927 miles (4,878km)
Period of revolution: 0.24 Earth-years
Daytime temperature: 600°F (316°C)
Discovery: Known since ancient times
Notable features: Occasional phases*

Venus

*Average distance from the sun: 65 million miles
    (108.2 million km)
Equatorial diameter: 7,262 miles (12,104km)
Period of revolution: 0.62 Earth-years
Daytime temperature: 867°F (464°C)
Discovery: Known since ancient times
Notable features: Cloud-covered; occasional phases*

Earth

*Average distance from the sun: 93 million miles
    (149.6 million km)*
Equatorial diameter: 7,654 miles (12,756km)
Period of revolution: 1 Earth-year
Daytime temperature: 60°F (16°C)
Discovery: Known since ancient times
Notable features: Blue oceans, white clouds

*Earth (left), Mercury (top right), and Venus (bottom right)
provided by NASA.*

© NASA

© Earl Young/FPG International

Mars

Average distance from the sun: 137 million miles
(227.9 million km)
Equatorial diameter: 4,072 miles (6,787km)
Period of revolution: 1.88 Earth-years
Daytime temperature: 50°F (10°C)
Discovery: Known since ancient times
Notable features: Orange surface, dark markings,
white polar caps

Jupiter

Average distance from the sun: 467 million miles
(778.4 million km)
Equatorial diameter: 85,680 miles (142,800km)
Period of revolution: 11.86 Earth-years
Daytime temperature: −184°F (−120°C)
Discovery: Known since ancient times
Notable features: Colorful cloud bands, Great Red Spot,
four bright moons

Mars (below) and
Jupiter (right) provided
by NASA.

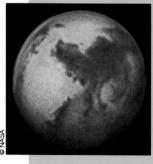

Saturn

*Average distance from the sun: 854 million miles
    (1,423.6 million km)*
Equatorial diameter: 75,100 miles (125,170km)
Period of revolution: 29.46 Earth-years
Daytime temperature: −291°F (−144°C)
Discovery: Known since ancient times
Notable features: Ring system

Uranus

*Average distance from the sun: 1,720 million miles
    (2,866 million km)*
Equatorial diameter: 30,720 miles (51,200km)
Period of revolution: 84.01 Earth-years
Daytime temperature: −344°F (−173°C)
Discovery: Herschel, 1781
Notable features: None

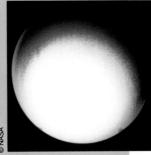

*Saturn (left) and
Uranus (below)
provided by NASA.*

© NASA

© NASA

Neptune

Average distance from the sun: 2,693 million miles (4,844.4 million km)
Equatorial diameter: 29,160 miles (48,600km)
Period of revolution: 164.79 Earth-years
Daytime temperature: −357°F (−181°C)
Discovery: Adams and Leverrier, 1846
Notable features: None

Pluto

Average distance from the sun: 3,544 million miles (5,906.2 million km)
Equatorial diameter: 1,380 miles (2,300km)
Period of revolution: 247.69 Earth-years
Daytime temperature: −396°F (−202°C)
Discovery: Tombaugh, 1930
Notable features: None

Neptune (below left) and Pluto (below right) provided by NASA.

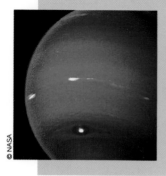

Chapter 14

Deep-Sky Objects

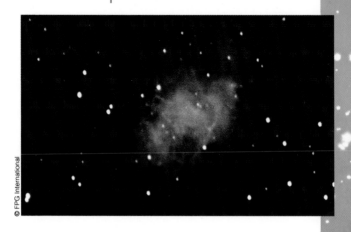

© FPG International

The stars lie far beyond the planets of our solar system. On a clear night, you can see thousands of them with the naked eye. Every single one is part of our Milky Way Galaxy.

We often think of the Milky Way as just the hazy band of light that steams overhead on dark nights. But this is just the central disk of our galaxy. If you gaze along this band with binoculars or a small telescope, you will discover millions more stars invisible to the eye alone.

Above: The Crab Nebula (also known as M1) is located in the constellation of Taurus. It is the remnant of a supernova explosion that occurred more than 930 years ago.

Observers in the Northern Hemisphere get their best views of the Milky Way in the direction of the constellation Cygnus, the Swan. Those south of the Earth's equator will find the viewing spectacular toward the constellation of Sagittarius.

Along with the Milky Way, dozens of "deep-sky objects" are also visible. Deep-sky objects are open or globular clusters of stars, diffuse or planetary nebulae, or spiral or elliptical galaxies. They are extremely far from us. Very faint and difficult to find, they are some of the most beautiful and majestic sights in the night sky. However, you could be disappointed by your first views of these objects, particularly if you expect to see the spectacular colorful and swirling images visible in photographs taken with the world's largest telescopes.

To observe deep-sky objects properly, you must have a lot of light-gathering power. Many deep-sky objects can be seen with telescopes 3 or 4 inches (7.5 or 10cm) in diameter, but larger instruments will provide much better views. Since these objects are faint and diffuse, they can often not be seen at all with high magnifications. Low or medium powers show them best.

In addition to light-gathering power, viewing deep-sky objects relies upon a good dark sky, far from the devastation of light pollution. In fact, most deep-sky objects will not be visible at all if the sky is not black. Others can be seen in bright skies, but their contrast is so low that much of their detail is lost from view.

Averted vision may also be necessary to see structure within some deep-sky objects—or even to see the objects themselves. As a result, these objects all appear as a greenish gray color. Still, no photograph can ever capture the feeling of seeing one of these distant celestial wonders firsthand.

Messier's List

Some of the brightest and most famous of deep-sky objects have been given proper names: the Crab Nebula, the Andromeda Galaxy, and the Double Cluster in Perseus. All, however, can be designated by catalog numbers. The Orion Nebula, for example, is also known as NGC 1976 (the 1,976th entry in the New General Catalog), and also as M42 (the 42nd object in the Messier Catalog).

Those objects most easily accessible to beginning stargazers are compiled in the Messier Catalog, named for Charles Messier, a French comet hunter of the eighteenth century. Messier knew that comets first appeared as faint, fuzzy blotches of light among the stars. Since comets orbited the sun, Messier also knew that they should appear to move among the stars over several nights' time. Messier sought to identify these comets.

Every time Messier found one of these hazy blotches of light in the sky, he made a note of it and watched carefully for its motion. More often than not, however, the object never moved, but appeared fixed to the starry vault. Messier became so frustrated with all his false comet discoveries that he began to compile a list of these objects so that they would not be mistaken for comets.

Ironically, Messier is not known for his comet discoveries at all, but for his list of 103 "nuisance" objects. Published in 1784, that famous list is known as the Messier Catalog, and now contains 109 such objects. Furthermore, since Messier used only a small telescope for his work, all of his catalog entries are within the range of beginning instruments. In fact, these entries are among the most spectacular sights in our sky.

Interstellar Clouds

Located just below the belt of Orion, the Hunter, the Orion Nebula (M42) is the most spectacular deep-sky object in the heavens. It shines as the hunter's sword, and is visible even to the naked eye. Northern Hemisphere observers can find the Orion Nebula on the winter star map on page 31; those in the Southern Hemisphere can find it on the summer star map on page 33. The Orion Nebula is marked with a "+" located in the lower half of the constellation.

Through a pair of binoculars, the Orion Nebula looks like a patch of light surrounding several stars. But

The Orion Nebula is perhaps one of the most spectacular deep-sky objects visible through a small telescope.

with a small telescope you can see wisps of luminous gas and dust stretching out across the entire field of view. At the nebula's center lies a compact grouping of four bluish white stars known as the Trapezium. These stars illuminate the cloud from within and make it visible to us 1,500 light-years away.

The Orion Nebula is one of many such clouds in which new stars are continually being born. Clumps of material collapse under their own weight, and when their internal temperatures rise high enough to begin nuclear fusion, they ignite and shine brightly across space. The Orion Nebula is one of the most prolific star-forming regions in our galaxy—a veritable stellar nursery. But the star birth process takes hundreds of thousands, even millions of years to occur, so you won't see it happen in your telescope.

Not all nebulae are sites of stellar birth, but are actually remnants of stellar death. Located 2,300 light-years away in the direction of the constellation Lyra, the Harp, lies one such nebula: the Ring Nebula (M57).

To a small backyard telescope, the Ring Nebula appears as a tiny gray smoke ring among the stars. If the sky is polluted with city lights, you may need to use averted vision even to find this object. But if the sky is dark, the Ring Nebula is quite easy to see.

This "ring" is actually a shell that was blown off from a star in its final gasp of life ages ago. The star itself—visible right at the center of the ring, but only through large telescopes—is believed to have once been much like our sun. If any life had originated and evolved on planets near this star, it most certainly is gone now.

Astronomers believe our sun will react as this ancient star did some 5 billion years in the future, when it, too, exhausts its supply of hydrogen fuel and blasts its atmosphere into space.

Star Clusters and Spiral Galaxies

Located in Taurus, one of the brightest constellations, is perhaps the most famous star cluster of all: the Pleiades (M45). Also known as the Seven Sisters because observers with good eyes can see seven stars without optical aid, this cluster appears to burst into hundreds of stars when viewed through a small telescope. Most of the stars in this cluster are hot, young bluish white stars; on a clear, dark night, they seem to sparkle like diamonds set on black velvet. The Pleiades is considered an "open" cluster, since its stars are bound loosely by mutual gravitation.

Long-exposure photographs show wisps of dust surrounding the stars of this cluster. This suggests that they are relatively young, perhaps only a few hundred million years old, and that this dust is material left over from their birth. Small telescopes do not show this dust, however.

Not all clusters are open. In the direction of the constellation of Hercules shines a distant cluster of thou-

Appearing as a very tiny and eerie smoke ring among the stars, the Ring Nebula shines in the constellation of Lyra, the Harp.

sands of stars. This cluster is so compact that it appears as a globe of stars—hence its name, "globular" cluster. This is the Globular Cluster in Hercules (M13).

Only a hundred or so globular clusters are known to astronomers. These clusters are among the oldest objects in the Milky Way Galaxy, and appear to form a halo around its center, which is located behind the constellation of Sagittarius. Telescopes larger than 4 inches (10cm) across are needed to distinguish individual stars in globular clusters, but these phenomena are still quite spectacular even with small backyard instruments.

Also visible on autumn or winter evenings from the Northern Hemisphere is another interesting deep-sky object, the Andromeda Galaxy (M31). This spiral galaxy is similar to, but larger than, the Milky Way. The Andromeda Galaxy can be easily found on your star map between Pegasus and Cassiopeia.

This galaxy appears to the naked eye as an elongated blob of light on dark nights. When viewed with binoculars or a telescope, it appears as an even larger hazy elliptical blob. What you are actually seeing is only the central region of this galaxy. The outlying areas, where the spiral pattern lies, are much too faint to be seen with backyard telescopes.

What is amazing, however, is that the Andromeda Galaxy is the most distant object we can see with the naked eye—even though it is located 2 million light-years away. That means that the light that hits your eye has been traveling through space since long before humans walked the Earth.

While Andromeda is the only galaxy visible to the naked eye from the Northern Hemisphere, Southern Hemisphere observers can actually see two galaxies: the Large and Small Magellanic Clouds (LMC and SMC). The LMC and the SMC are actually satellite galaxies to the Milky Way and appear as two amorphous patches of light among the stars of the Southern Hemisphere.

Globular clusters are well within range of small telescopes. Their many stars look like moths hovering around a bright streetlight.

While they are indeed distant galaxies, they lie merely 190,000 light-years from us.

These three objects, the Andromeda Galaxy, and the Large and Small Magellanic clouds, are only three of many hundreds of similar galaxies visible to anyone with a backyard telescope, a detailed star map showing their positions, a dark sky, and plenty of patience.

The Andromeda Galaxy is one of the Milky Way's closest neighboring galaxies.

Courtesy of Meade Instruments

A Universe for Everyone

The beauty of astronomy is that the entire laboratory is right outside your back door, and it's one of the few fields to which amateurs can make a direct and immediate contribution. You don't need fancy or expensive equipment to make an impact.

Suppose, for example, you have an interest in cameras. You may wish to develop astrophotography

Above: The Aurora Borealis, which is often visible to observers in the Northern Hemisphere, occurs when electrically charged particles from the sun cause our atmosphere to glow.

as a hobby. Some amateurs have even begun to use CCD cameras and computers to develop image-enhancement techniques. Others just like to get outdoors in the wilderness with a camera and a tripod and try their hand at photographing sunsets or constellations.

Maybe your night skies are illuminated by too much light pollution to do a good job observing the stars or deep-sky objects. You might enjoy sketching or photographing the moon or planets. Or, if you enjoy watching the sun (safely, of course!), there are organizations that keep daily tabs on sunspot numbers and types. This information is compiled by the organization and ultimately helps scientists understand the sun and its influence on our Earth.

Perhaps you'd like to search for previously undiscovered comets. This is an area that requires patience, but is one in which amateurs make virtually all the discoveries.

Or meteor showers might be your interest. Gathering a group of amateurs to view meteor showers and planning a concerted observation program can help determine the size and structure of meteor swarms in space as well as help astronomers predict better from year to year what type of shower to expect.

Whichever avenue you choose—whether you prefer to casually glance up toward the sky and recognize constellations or to carry out a more detailed research project—amateur astronomy is an exciting and constantly changing endeavor, a hobby that will challenge and inspire you throughout your life.

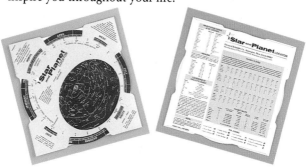

Glossary

Altitude-azimuth mounting: *A telescope mounting in which one axis is parallel to the ground and the other is perpendicular to it.*

Altitude: *The height of something above the horizon; usually measured in degrees.*

Asterism: *A group of stars that can be made to form a familiar shape. See* **Constellation.**

Averted vision: *A technique of using the edges of the retina to see very faint objects in the sky.*

Azimuth: *The measure of an object's position along the horizon; usually measured in degrees eastward from the north.*

Bolide: *A brilliant meteor that smokes, whistles, or explodes during its fall through the atmosphere. See* **Meteor.**

Comet: *A chunk of ice with a long, glowing tail that sometimes appears in the sky.*

Conjunction: *When two celestial bodies lie almost along the same line of sight.*

Constellation: *An arbitrary area of the sky that represents a person, thing, or animal from ancient times. See* **Asterism.**

Corona: *The outer atmosphere of the sun seen only during a total solar eclipse.*

Dark adaptation: *A condition of "night vision" in which your eyes have become adjusted to the darkness.*

Degree: *An angular measure equal to $\frac{1}{360}$ of a circle. One degree of the horizon is about the width of your little finger held at arm's length.*

Equatorial mounting: *A telescope mounting in which one axis is parallel to the Earth's axis of rotation and the other is perpendicular to it.*

Field of view: *The area of the sky visible through binoculars or a telescope.*

Falling Star: *See* Meteor.

Galaxy: *A collection of hundreds of billions of stars, star clusters, and clouds of dust and gas. The Milky Way is a galaxy.*

Globular star cluster: *A tightly packed ball of thousands or millions of stars.*

Horizon: *The imaginary line that joins the sky and the ground. The true horizon can be seen only on the open ocean.*

Light pollution: *Light from streetlights and cities that shines into the sky and makes it difficult to see faint stars.*

Lunar eclipse: *A phenomenon that occurs when the moon passes into the shadow of the Earth and disappears temporarily.*

Magnification: *The apparent increase in size from an object to its image.*

Magnitude: *The brightness of a star as we see it. A 1st-magnitude star is as bright as a candle flame ¼ mile (0.4 km) away.*

Meteor: *A speck of dust that burns up as it falls into our atmosphere.*

Meteorite: *A chunk of iron or rock that has fallen from space.*

Meteoroid: *A piece of dust, rock, or iron tumbling through space.*

Milky Way: *The hazy band of light we see in the nighttime sky. The Milky Way forms the plane of the galaxy in which we live.*

Nebula: *A cloud of gas and dust in space.*

Objective: *In a reflector telescope, the primary mirror. In a refractor telescope or binoculars, the front, or principal, lens.*

Opposition: *When a celestial body lies on the opposite side of the sky from the sun. The full moon, for example, always occurs at opposition.*

Penumbra: *The light outer shadow of any solid body.*

Radiant: *The point in the heavens from which meteor showers seem to emerge.*

Reflector telescope: *An instrument that uses a mirror to gather light from the sky and focus it into an image for us to magnify and study.*

Refractor telescope: *An instrument that uses a lens to gather light from the sky and focus it into an image for us to magnify and study.*

Rich-field telescope: *A telescope with a very wide field of view.*

Scintillation: *The movement of a star's image caused by the turbulent atmosphere around us. Also known as twinkling.*

Shooting star: *See* **Meteor.**

Solar eclipse: *A phenomenon that occurs when the moon passes between the Earth and the Sun, temporarily blocking the sunlight.*

Star cluster: *A family of stars held together by gravity.*

Star hopping: *The trick astronomers use to find a star or group of stars by using other stars as "pointers."*

Sunspots: *Dark spots on the face of the sun that appear to move about and change as the sun rotates.*

Twinkling: *See* **Scintillation.**

Umbra: *The dark inner shadow of a solid body.*

Zenith: *The point in our sky that lies directly overhead.*

Zodiacal light: *A triangular haze of light that appears in our sky. Caused by the reflected light from tiny particles along the plane of our solar system.*

Helpful Calculations

Calculating Star Trail Lengths

Star trails will appear to be different lengths, depending on the lens and time exposure you use, and the star's position in the sky. A star farthest from the celestial poles will show a maximum length. To calculate the maximum length of a star trail on your film, use the following equation:

$$\text{Length of trail on film (millimeters)} = \frac{\text{Lens focal length (millimeters)} \times \text{Time exposure (minutes)}}{5{,}816}$$

Calculating the Magnification of an Eyepiece-Telescope Combination

Every eyepiece-telescope combination gives a different magnification. To determine yours, you must first determine the focal lengths of the eyepiece and telescope, which are usually written on their sides or in the instruction manuals. Then use this equation:

$$\text{Magnification} = \frac{\text{Focal length of telescope (millimeters)}}{\text{Focal length of eyepiece (millimeters)}}$$

Calculating the Relative-Light-Efficiency of Binoculars

The relative-light-efficiency of binoculars, or RLE, determines how efficiently you are using light. In astronomy, where light is scarce, getting the RLE as close to 1 as possible is important. To determine this, you must use both the objective diameter and the magnifying power of the instrument. Both are written on the binoculars.

$$RLE = \frac{\text{Diameter (millimeters)}}{\text{Magnification} \times \text{Magnification}}$$

Calculating the Maximum Magnification of a Telescope

Every telescope has a limit to how much it can magnify before the image degrades. Usually, that limit is around 50 power per inch of diameter or about 20 power per millimeter of diameter. To calculate the limit, use the following equation:

Maximum magnification = Telescope diameter × 50
(inches)

Maximum magnification = Telescope diameter × 20
(millimeters)

Calculating Angular Widths of Celestial Objects

To measure the angular size of a celestial object, or to determine its altitude, azimuth, or speed across the sky, you can use parts of your hand (little finger, thumb, or fist), or make yourself an "angular" ruler from cardboard. To determine the approximate angular size of any measuring tool, measure its width and distance from your eye. You can use any dimensions you wish (inches, millimeters, centimeters, etc.), with the following equation:

$$\text{Angular size (degrees)} = 55 \times \frac{\text{Linear width}}{\text{Distance from eye}}$$

Recommended Reading

Clairborne, Robert. *The Summer Stargazer*. New York: Coward, McCann & Geoghegan, Inc., 1975.

Covington, Michael. *Astrophotography for the Amateur*. New York: Cambridge University Press, 1991.

Eastman Kodak. *Astrophotography Basics*. Rochester, NY: Eastman Kodak, 1988.

Harrington, Sherwood. *Selecting a First Telescope*. San Francisco, CA: Astronomical Society of the Pacific, 1988.

Mallas, John, and Evered Kreimer. *The Messier Album*. Cambridge, MA: Sky Publishing Corporation, 1978.

Martin, Martha Evans, and Donald Howard Menzel. *The Friendly Stars*. New York: Dover Publications, Inc., 1966.

Mayall, R. Newton, and Margaret Mayall. *Skyshooting: Photography for the Amateur Astronomer*. New York: Dover Publications, Inc., 1968.

Nourse, Alan E. *The Backyard Astronomer*. New York: Franklin Watts, Inc., 1973.

Peltier, Leslie. *Starlight Nights*. Cambridge, MA: Sky Publishing Corporation, 1980.

Zim, Herbert S., and Robert H. Baker. *Stars*. New York: Golden Press, 1985.

International Magazines

Astronomy Now, Intra House, 193 Uxbridge Road, London W12 9RA, England

Royal Astronomical Society of Canada Handbook, RASC, 130 Dupont Street, Toronto, Ontario M5R IVZ

Sky & Telescope, Sky Publishing Corporation, 40-50-51 Bay State Road, Cambridge, MA 02238

Astronomy Organizations

Australia

Astronomy Society of Victoria, Box 1059J GPO, Melbourne 3001

Astronomy Society of NSW, Box 208, Eastwood, NSW 2122

Canada

Royal Astronomical Society of Canada, 124 Merton Street, Toronto, Ontario M4S 2Z2

Canadian Amateur Astronomers, 417 Foch Avenue, Windsor, Ontario N8X 2W2

England

British Astronomical Association, Burlington House, Piccadilly, London W1V 9AG

British Interplanetary Society, 12 Bessborough GDS, London SW1V 2JJ

France

Association Française d'Astronomie, 115 rue de Charenton, Paris 75012

Société d'Astronomie Populaire, 9 rue Ozenne HTE Garonne, Toulouse 31400

United States

Astronomical Society of the Pacific, 390 Ashton Avenue, San Francisco, CA 94112

The Planetary Society, 65 North Catalina Avenue, Pasadena, CA 91106

Index